"The secret hardships, trials, and early life ex mate/roommate and lifelong friend I though of a young girl born in rural East Tennessee in the 1940s, combination of courage, determination, and resourcefulness, rose from poverty to become a prestigious and successful OB/GYN in Chattanooga, Tennessee—close to where she grew up. The qualities of responsibility, compassion, and love were never questioned as Phyllis 'mothered' Bozo, her curious puppy. As you follow the trials, disappointments, losses, and joys of this young woman, you start to realize that when one is surrounded by a loving and caring family that believes in you, no mountain is too tall to climb!"

Dana Wallace, M.D.
Allergy and Immunology Specialist
Ft. Lauderdale, Fla.

"This is a story that needs to be told. Teenagers need to hear that with persistence and courage they can overcome modest backgrounds. And extended families and teachers need to recognize how important they are. It was a pleasure and honor to serve patients with this outstanding clinician and leader."

B. W. Ruffner, M.D.
Oncologist
Signal Mountain, Tenn.

"*Climbing Mountains* is a fine work based on the life of Dr. Phyllis Miller. While still in high school, Dr. Miller's mother and father both passed away. She persevered and graduated from Polk County High School, Tennessee Tech, and the University of Tennessee Medical School. She came to Chattanooga to practice medicine and is now one of Chattanooga's leading physicians. Along the way, she has headed up the Chattanooga-Hamilton County Medical Society and the Tennessee Medical Association. Her life is one of perseverance, courage, and accomplishment."

John Guerry
Retired Business Executive
Chattanooga, Tenn.

"There are very special individuals who, despite many reasons and excuses to give up, choose to look forward, accept challenges, and face the odds in pursuit of a dream or goal. Phyllis Miller is unequivocally one of those people. During a time and under circumstances where the common expectation of her future would have been much more traditional, she chose to follow her heart, create her own path, and define her future. Demonstrating a solid plan executed with a true north grounded in the principles of excellence, hard work, humility, compassion, and kindness—no matter how daunting the challenge—is one of Miller's most valuable legacies. *Climbing Mountains* captures a few highlights of Phyllis Miller's remarkable personal and professional journey defined by persistence, personality, and adventure."

Rachel Miller-Tester
Aviation Professional
Chattanooga, Tenn.

"Phyllis Miller is a physician, community servant and leader of physicians, and has been throughout her exemplary career. As the first woman to lead the Chattanooga-Hamilton County Medical Society and the Tennessee Medical Association, Dr. Miller has been a role model and mentor for many. As a beloved physician, she is considered one of the finest advocates for women's health care. Her accomplishments are all the more remarkable when you understand the obstacles and challenges she had to overcome early in life. Her biography is a testament to tenacity, intellect, and sheer force of will as she journeyed from a small rural home without electricity and loss of both parents as a teenager to broad recognition as a physician leader and healer."

Rae Young Bond
Chief Executive Officer
Chattanooga-Hamilton County Medical Society

CLIMBING
MOUNTAINS

Dr. Phyllis Miller's Onward, Upward Journey

LYNELLE MASON

© 2020
Published in the United States by Nurturing Faith Inc., Macon GA,
www.nurturingfaith.net.

Nurturing Faith is the book publishing arm of Good Faith Media (goodfaithmedia.org).

Library of Congress Cataloging-in-Publication Data is available.

ISBN: 978-1-63528-102-6

A portion of the proceeds from the sale of Climbing Mountains will be donated to the Polk County Education Foundation to provide college scholarships for deserving students in Polk County, Tennessee.

I would like to thank Lynelle Mason for taking on this project of writing a book about my life. It has been a labor of love. My family and I will be forever grateful to her for this treasure.

—Phyllis Edwards Miller

I would like to dedicate Climbing Mountains *to all of America's medical workers—past, present, and future—who daily risk their lives for others. During this pandemic we've come to know as Covid-19, I especially want them to know they're our heroes. Whether taking out the trash or working in a lab seeking a cure, each worker is vital to our recovery.*

—Lynelle Mason

Contents

Foreword

I have known Phyllis Miller since she was a medical student rotating on my service in surgery at the University of Tennessee College of Medicine in Memphis, where I was a senior surgery resident. Our association has continued through the decades, as we located to and practiced in the same city for most of our professional lives. My regard for her is such that you could describe me as a charter member of her fan club.

So, I am pleased with this written account of an unusually talented, charismatic, and brilliant woman who has left her mark not only on the lives of hundreds if not thousands of patients but also on organized healthcare through her unselfish and sensitive but forceful leadership.

As someone who also grew up in a poor, rural area in East Tennessee, the account of Phyllis' early life in rural, agrarian Polk County gave me a pleasant déjà vu experience. In addition to the advantage of her close-knit family, the recollection of the helping hands extended by members of her community and especially high school teachers demonstrates some of the huge advantages of growing up in rural America.

While the offering of such help by family, friends and community/school leaders is admirable, it is also essential that individuals have the intellect and drive to take those opportunities and make the most of them. Phyllis Edwards Miller took the opportunity and made the most of it. Reading this book gives added understanding of what shaped the life of such an outstanding woman, physician, healthcare leader, mother, and friend.

I enjoyed reading the history of her education, especially college and medical school. It points out the intense determination Phyllis had. Many of my family members have also attended Tennessee Technological University, and have enjoyed similar support and direction in their lives from special individuals at that school. I remember Phyllis as a medical school student in Memphis taking full advantage of clinical learning opportunities, unflinching in her pursuit of medical education.

While the leadership positions and other responsibilities she has achieved are impressive, perhaps the most important achievement for Doctor Miller is the impact she has had on the lives of so many patients and therefore their families. It has been my privilege to work as her colleague and evaluate and treat many of her patients. Her clinical ability and pragmatic, realistic evaluations of patients and their problems have always been impressive. In addition, her personal relationship with and caring for those patients was and is unusually dedicated. She doesn't just know and understand their health problems; she knows them as a person.

Phyllis Miller, M.D., has been a trailblazer for women in medicine. The number of firsts she has achieved—including first woman president of the Chattanooga Hamilton County Medical Society, first woman chief of staff at Erlanger Medical Center, and first woman president of the Tennessee Medical Association—opened the doors for many other women to follow suit. She has proved that gender is not a determinant in doing an excellent job.

Along the way Phyllis has received several accolades for her career, including first woman to receive the Erlanger Baroness Lifetime Achievement Award and either the first or one of the first to receive the University of Tennessee College of Medicine Distinguished Alumnus Award. She also believes in giving back to others.

Twenty years ago, in gratitude to her parents for her upbringing and to the community that nurtured her, Phyllis labored to create the Polk County Education Fund that awards college scholarships to deserving students—33 at last count.

While I have benefited greatly from the professional relationship I have shared with Phyllis Miller, most importantly I appreciate her friendship. I am truly blessed that she has touched my life.

Phillip Burns, M.D.
Professor and Chairman, Department of Surgery
University of Tennessee College of Medicine, Chattanooga, Tenn.

Introduction

The land inhabited by the Edwards family in 1947, two years after the end of World War II, bore a striking resemblance to the primitive surroundings in 1848 when it was home to the Cherokee Indians. This wild mountainous area in Polk County, Tennessee—nestled near Sheeds Creek and surrounded by yellow poplars, oaks, and towering pines—was destined to birth a very special child.

The box-shaped house put together by Arthur Edwards was subdivided into a living room, kitchen, two bedrooms, and an attic. The living room had a dilapidated, faded green couch; Lela B. Edwards' rocking chair; and a wood stove that became the family's main source of heat in the chilly winter months. The pipe of the stove connected to the chimney in the middle of the house.

Although President Franklin D. Roosevelt's Rural Electrification Act (REA) was established in 1935, it had yet to come to the southeastern hinterlands of Tennessee. The Edwards' farmstead had no electricity or running water. Indoor plumbing didn't exist, and necessary jobs required a trip to the outhouse. Nearby Sheeds Creek and a mountain spring provided drinking water, refrigeration, and water for general household tasks.

The family's outlet to the outside world was a battery-powered radio, a weekly subscription to *Grit Magazine*, and a 1940 Chevrolet—an old rattletrap with a mind of its own.

As shades of night began creeping over their farmstead, Lela, now great with child, began crumbling up old newspapers. Using the newsprint, she wiped the smut from the glass lamps that resided in each room of her house. Then she filled the base of the lamps with kerosene, trimmed their wicks, and lit them. Meanwhile, Arthur, returning from the fields, began washing up for supper.

Suddenly, Lela shouted: "Arthur, get me to the hospital! Our baby is ready to be born."

Arthur hurriedly splashed water over his grimy hands and dashed to the car. He tossed Lela's sheepskin coverlet over the open and corroded floorboard and then pumped hard on the starter key. Nothing happened. He waited a couple of minutes and tried again. Still the car didn't start. A self-styled mechanic, Arthur leaped under the car, twisted a few wires, and tried once more to start the engine. He drew a heavy sigh of relief when the motor began sputtering.

Lela groped her way out the back door and climbed into the car on the passenger's side. Arthur made a quick stop at his brother's house to drop off their young son, Charles. Their next stop would be Cleveland, some 26 miles away. Lela tried to muffle her labor pains as they jostled along the first 14 miles over a rough-shod, dusty dirt road. The final passage road was somewhat smoother. Upon their arrival at the hospital, an attendant with a wheelchair rushed Lela inside.

On March 28, 1947, Lela Edwards gave birth to her second child, Phyllis.

The Edwards Homeplace

Early Childhood
1947-1953

Charles and Phyllis

Sibling Rivalry

On their way home from the hospital, Lela and Arthur stopped to pick up their 16-month-old son Charles, who jumped up and down while clapping his hands when he saw his parents. Charles took one look at the new intruder, however, and groaned in his toddler language, "A sister? Can't we exchange her for a boy?"

It wasn't long before Phyllis with her cherubic face, blond hair, and blue eyes began carving out her special niche. She doted on the outlandish displays of adulation she received from her parents and kinfolk, and early on took note of the quick temper of her brother.

Meanwhile, the months and years of her early childhood passed swiftly. Phyllis, the youngest child in the Edwards clan was surrounded by a slew of young male relatives. Phyllis readily joined her brother and cousins in whatever caught their fancy. She was determined to do everything they did. She had no use for prissy girl clothes and was most comfortable in a pair of blue jeans. If her peers climbed trees, so did Phyllis. If they played baseball and chose her last, she still played ball.

Phyllis couldn't resist messing around with her brother's prized possessions. She was especially fascinated with Charles' fishing rod. When she spied it lying on the grass near Sheeds Creek, her curiosity won the battle. She picked up the rod but quickly laid it back down. *If Charles finds me messing with his fishing rod and reel, he'll kill me!* Then glancing around and seeing no one, she picked it up again. Pretending she was fishing, she cast the rod. Much to her dismay, the line became entangled in a nearby tree.

Phyllis yanked and yanked on the line, but it refused to yield. She took one last look at the mangled line and began wringing her hands. Then she took off running and hid among a copse of trees.

It wasn't long until she spied Charles sauntering toward the disaster sight. Suddenly she heard a yell that could be heard for miles. Phyllis began biting her nails and sobbing. *Charles' rod and reel are ruined, and it's all my fault.* But then her eyes lit up. *Maybe if I help him get it out of the tree, he'll forgive me.*

"Charles! Charles!" she yelled as she rushed to his side. "I don't know what happened. I picked up the rod to cast the line and when I looked up, your fishing line was in the top of this oak tree. I tried but I couldn't pry the fishing line from the branches of the tree. Please, please forgive me!"

Charles spit on the ground. "Stop your blubbering! Climb the tree with me, and we'll see if we can free the line." The two of them worked for well over an hour before the line became free.

Phyllis turned to leave, but Charles grabbed her arm. "Not so fast." Grinning, he said, "You're going with me to show Daddy what you did. I'm looking forward to watching you squirm when I tell him what his precious daughter did to my rod and reel."

Phyllis followed timidly behind Charles as they made their way back home and into the living room where Daddy was resting. Charles tossed the knotted fishing line onto Daddy's lap. Yelling loudly, he said, "I thought you'd like to see this! Phyllis has ruined the line attached to my rod and reel. I'll never get it untangled."

His nostrils flared and he shot daggers at Phyllis, who had slid over on the couch until she was within an earshot of Daddy. Never raising her voice, she said, "I was only trying to catch us a fish for supper."

Daddy shook his head in disbelief and waited a while before he spoke. "I'll unknot your fishing line, provided you teach your sister how to cast a line and fish."

That wasn't what Charles wanted to hear, but he knew better than to sass his daddy. His face turned red, and he bit his lower lip. A few hours elapsed before he cornered Phyllis in the backyard. He shoved her until she lay sprawled on the ground. Shaking his finger, he warned, "When you least expect it I'm going to make you pay for messing up my rod and reel."

Charles turned on his heels and left. Phyllis got up and dusted off her jeans. She shuttered. *Even Daddy isn't clever enough to save me from Charles' wrath. Oh, my! He's such a meanie.*

Charles, still licking his wounds, was quick to seek retaliation against Phyllis.

Phyllis glanced out the living room window and watched as Charles and her cousins took turns riding Tarzan, the family horse. Taking giant steps, she raced to join them. Placing her arms squarely on her hips, she demanded: "Why didn't someone tell me you were taking turns riding Tarzan?"

The boys giggled and Charles poked her with his fist. "Riding a horse is for boys only."

One of her cousins said, "Maybe, just maybe when you're five years older you might be able to take a ride."

Phyllis didn't linger to argue. Instead she went directly to her father, who was busy mending his tools at his blacksmith shop. Phyllis quickly donned her pouting face, the one that almost never failed to evoke Daddy's sympathy.

"My goodness, Phyllis! What's happened? Why the long face?"

Phyllis cooed, "Daddy, the boys are taking turns riding Tarzan and they say I can't have a turn."

Daddy laid aside his working tools. "Come with me. I'll see that you get to ride Tarzan."

One of the fellows motioned to Charles. "Here comes Trouble, and she's bringing your daddy over to champion her side."

Daddy cleared his voice, "Charles, what's this I hear about you refusing to let your sister ride Tarzan?"

Charles stomped his right foot and shouted, "Gee whiz, Daddy. Isn't there anything I can do without her horning in?"

Daddy placed his hand on Charles' shoulder. "If you know what's good for you, you'll lower your voice. You either let Phyllis have a turn riding Tarzan or I'll put Tarzan in her stall and no one will be riding." Daddy hesitated before adding, "Have I made myself clear?"

The boys nodded and exclaimed, "Yes, sir, very clear."

One of Phyllis' cousins beckoned to her. "Come and I'll help you get on the saddle."

Phyllis accepted his offer, and Daddy returned to his work shed.

As soon as Daddy was out of sight, Charles winked to his buddies and slapped Tarzan on his rump. Sure enough, the horse headed straight toward a low-hanging limb of a sturdy oak.

Before Phyllis knew what had happened, she was on the ground, rubbing her rear end. She glanced around and spied the boys whooping it up.

Not to be outdone and with her eyes sparkling with determination, Phyllis exclaimed, "I'll show them!" She quickly remounted Tarzan and trotted along as if nothing had happened.

Phyllis early on displayed the trait that when you want to do something, you don't take no for an answer.

Pet Mania

While Daddy and his first cousin Glen were building the family a new house, Charles informed Glen, "I know how to say 'shit.'" Glen held his hand over his mouth to keep from laughing out loud.

Not to be outdone, Phyllis tugged on Glen's arm and told him, "I can say 'shit,' too."

Glen laid aside his hammer. "Hmm, that's interesting. Where did the two of you hear that word?"

Charles and Phyllis answered at the same time. "Every time Mama gets upset. she says 'shit!'"

"Yeah," said Charles. "Like the time Phyllis and I found some black-and-white furry animals on the edge of the woods."

Phyllis, nodding her head, interjected, "We brought them to Mama and asked her if we could keep them as pets."

"I thought Mama's eyes would pop out of her head," said Charles. "She kept mumbling to herself, 'shit, shit, shit.'"

Charles and Phyllis continued telling their story.

"Please, Mama, let us keep them. They're so cute," said Phyllis.

Mama pushed both of her hands outward. "Quick! Take those baby skunks back where you found them. People don't have skunks as pets!"

Charles, never one to accept "no" as an answer, asked, "Why not?"

"If those spotted skunks were a little older, you wouldn't be asking me such a question. Skunks can send out a spray from their rear ends that is horrible—and the smell stays around for a long, long time."

Phyllis and Charles reluctantly returned the furry black creatures with big white spots to where they found them. The baby skunks seemed relieved to be home and quickly vanished under a clump of bushes.

Morning, noon, and night Phyllis hounded her parents for a dog. "Please, pretty please!" she begged, "get me a dog. I'll feed her, bath her, and give her shots if she gets sick."

Phyllis was on the verge of asking one more time for a dog when Daddy announced in a strong voice: "Phyllis, I'm tired of hearing you beg us to get you a dog."

Phyllis swallowed hard and dropped her head. Daddy, showing a quirky smile, continued: "Our neighbor Jim has a litter of pups, and he's promised me we could have one of them. Child, grab your jacket and come with me. He's expecting us to pick up your puppy today."

Summer was meshing into fall, and the fiery red foliage of the maple trees dotted the landscape as Phyllis and her dad drove for several miles down the dust-laden road and finally through the small creek leading to Jim's homestead.

"Howdy, neighbor," said Jim. "You're lucky. Since you're the first to come for a puppy, I'll let you have your pick of the litter. Would you like a boy or girl dog?"

Phyllis tugged on Daddy's arm. "Tell him we want a girl dog." Her father and Jim exchanged smiles.

Meanwhile, Phyllis knelt down and stretched out her hands. Several puppies came running to sniff her out. One of the puppies lingered longer than the rest. Suddenly she planted a quick tongue kiss on Phyllis' nose.

"Daddy, did you see that?" asked Phyllis. "She gave me a kiss. It's settled. She's the puppy for me."

Clutching her puppy in her arms, Phyllis and Daddy got in the car and headed home. They hadn't traveled far when she asked, "Daddy, why is my puppy whimpering? It sounds like she's crying."

Daddy nodded his head. "She's crying because she misses her mama. Don't fret. In a few days she'll think you're her mother and she'll stop whimpering."

Phyllis sighed. "I hope she stops whimpering soon. I don't like for her to be sad."

As they neared home, Daddy said, "I need to do some plowing." After parking their car, he added, "This is a good time for you to introduce your puppy to the rest of the family."

Phyllis, knowing her daddy always kept his feelings to himself, hesitated and then did an unheard-of thing in their family: She threw her arms around Daddy's neck and shouted, "Thank you, Daddy. You've made me very happy!"

Daddy shrugged his shoulders and mumbled, "It doesn't take much to make you happy."

Mama saw them coming and ran to meet them. "See my puppy," said Phyllis. "Isn't she beautiful?"

Mama picked up the puppy and a warm stream of water began running down her arm. Mama laughed. "It looks like your puppy's kidneys are working fine.

Phyllis, you can't go around calling her 'Puppy' for the rest of her life. Let's give her a name."

Phyllis thought and thought. All at once she jumped to her feet. "I've got the perfect name for my puppy. Aunt Noonie read me a story about Bozo the clown. In the story Bozo is always getting into trouble. Let's name my puppy Bozo."

The evening shades of night were playing hide-and-seek when Daddy returned from the fields. "Where's Phyllis?" he asked.

"She's on the front porch with Bozo."

Daddy grinned. "Bozo? I thought Bozo was a clown."

Mama chuckled. "Phyllis says her puppy, like Bozo the clown, does funny things that makes her laugh."

Daddy ran his fingers through his hair and said, "I'll be back in a few minutes. Phyllis and I need to talk."

"Daddy," begged Phyllis, "can Bozo sleep with me tonight?'

Daddy cleared his throat. "Young lady, let's get something straight. You have a puppy, not a child. I'll fix her a box with a pallet, and Bozo can sleep under the porch."

Tears welled in Phyllis' eyes. "But, Daddy, look at her. She's so tiny and so lonesome for her mama."

Daddy paused. "If it will make you feel better, I'll sleep out here with her tonight."

"Can I join you, Daddy? If I'm up in my attic room and she's out here with you, I won't sleep a wink worrying about her."

Daddy threw up his hands in desperation. "Sure. Why not?"

Phyllis watched as Daddy made a bed for Bozo. When he had finished, she said, "Daddy, I think Bozo needs a little company." She ran inside and when she returned, she was clutching her favorite stuffed dog. She gently placed it inside Bozo's box home.

No sooner had they settled in for the night than Bozo began whimpering. Her whimpers became louder and louder. Phyllis turned to Daddy. "What do we do now?"

"Try getting her to nibble on your stuffed animal," answered Daddy.

Bozo responded by gnawing on the stuffed animal, but she soon deserted it. Phyllis reached over and began rubbing Bozo's tummy. The whimpering stopped!

When morning broke through the lofty East Tennessee woods, Daddy shook Phyllis. "Wake up, Phyllis. It's time to feed Bozo."

Phyllis yawned and blinked her sleep-encrusted eyes. "Being a parent is a big responsibility, isn't it, Daddy?"

Daddy chuckled. "You got that right!"

The months and years passed swiftly. One day while Phyllis and Bozo were walking near the deep woods, Bozo bolted into the underbrush. All Phyllis could see in the distance was a faint glimmer of a bushy gray tail weaving to and fro, with Bozo in hot pursuit. Soon, even that image became blurred.

Frowning, Phyllis hunkered down at the foot of a sturdy poplar tree to await Bozo's return. The wait grew longer and longer. As the shadows of darkness began gathering, Bozo still hadn't returned. Phyllis plodded home.

"Why are you so late for supper, and where's Bozo?" asked her mother.

Phyllis bit her lower lip. "Bozo decided to chase a squirrel. Mama, do you reckon she's hurt or has lost her way home?"

Mama laughed. "Chances are she's having a grand old time. Everyone except you has already eaten. Wash up and eat your dinner before it gets cold."

Phyllis drummed her fingers on the table and shoved her fried okra to the side of her plate. "Mama, excuse me. I don't feel hungry." As she stood to leave, she heard an incessant bark that grew louder and louder. Phyllis rushed outside. There stood Bozo with a dead squirrel dangling from her mouth. Bozo dropped her trophy at Phyllis' feet.

"Look at you!" cried Phyllis. "You silly old clown. Your long mane is full of burrs!" She turned to Mama. "What can I do?"

"Go to Daddy's shop and find the comb he uses on his horses. Meanwhile, I'll pour some cooking oil over the places where the burrs are lodged."

In a few minutes Phyllis returned with a big steel comb. "Good," said Mama. "Since Bozo trusts you, she'll let you get rid of the burrs. But don't take it personal if she nips at you. Gently run the comb over the areas covered with burrs."

For more than two hours Bozo stood still, without barking even once, until all the burrs were removed. "There!" said Phyllis as she hugged Bozo. "You're fit as a fiddle." Glancing down at the squirrel, Phyllis asked, "Mama, can you turn this critter into squirrel stew?"

Phyllis bonded with Bozo and felt Bozo was her responsibility, providing loving care for him.

Elementary School
1953-1960

School Days

Throughout the hot muggy days of summer, Phyllis pelted Daddy with questions about school. "What happens if I don't like school? Will my teacher like me? Can I wear jeans to school? Who will take care of Bozo while I'm gone? Does school start tomorrow?"

Daddy, wearing a despairing look, shook his head. "Phyllis, you're a basketful of questions! Yes, you can wear your jeans to school and if you listen to what your teachers tell you, study hard and turn in your homework, you won't have any problems with your teachers. As for Bozo, he'll be fine while you're away."

He scratched his head. "You're rushing this school-starting thing! School doesn't begin until the day after Labor Day."

Phyllis blinked her eyes. "Daddy, how much longer is it until Labor Day?"

"Wait here while I get a calendar." In a few minutes he returned. Pointing to August 15, he said, "This is where we are today." Then he flipped over to September 2 and said, "This is when school starts."

"But, Daddy," moaned Phyllis, "I want to go to school now!"

Daddy's eyes lit up. "I have an idea that will help you keep track of when you'll begin school. Every day I want you to put an "X" on the calendar days until you get to the first Monday in September. Do you think you can do that?"

Phyllis clapped her hands together and ran to find a pencil. Every day she added another "X" on the calendar until the day for school to begin was one day away. She found pleasure in charting the days until school started.

In 1953, World War II hero Dwight David Eisenhower became America's 34th president. That same year 6-year-old Phyllis Edwards made her venture to the outside world. To get to Ocoee Elementary School some 17 miles away, she and her brother would need to leave home by 7:00 a.m. They would not return home until 6:00 p.m.

Charles continued working overtime to dampen Phyllis' enthusiasm. "You don't know what you're wishing for," he exclaimed. "Day after day, week after week, month after month, it will be school, school, and more school! They don't give you time off to go hunting or fishing."

The next morning Phyllis was downstairs dressed and waiting before anyone in the family began stirring. Soon, Mama arrived. "Well, look at you! Is this a Sunday go-to-meeting day?"

Phyllis giggled. "Aw, Mama, quit teasing me. You know why I'm up so early. Do I look alright?"

Mama nodded her approval and began bustling around in the kitchen. Next, Daddy joined them. Last of all, Charles showed up wiping the sleep from his eyes and only partially dressed.

After they had all eaten a hearty breakfast Mama, with a faraway look in her eyes, hugged Phyllis and whispered, "I don't know how this is possible. It seems just yesterday I brought you home from the hospital ... my baby girl."

Phyllis twisted her hands together. "Mama, I'm so excited. I do hope my teacher likes me."

Phyllis and Charles waited until the bus passed their house, knowing it would soon turn around and come back for them. Clutching her five sheets of clean paper Daddy had allotted her, Phyllis grabbed Charles' hand and together they skipped down the lane toward the road near Sheeds Creek. When they arrived both of them turned for one final glimpse of home. They began jumping up and down as they saw Bozo bounding toward them. Behind Bozo was Daddy, huffing and puffing as he tried to catch Bozo.

"Bozo, go home!" shouted Phyllis. "You can't come with us."

Confused over what to do, Bozo stopped in her tracks, ducked her tail between her legs, and slowly turned around and went with Daddy.

Soon the school bus arrived, leaving in its wake a cloud of dust. Phyllis and Charles hopped aboard. Since they were the first ones on his route, the driver had to travel several miles before he began picking up the other children.

After Mr. Snyder, the bus driver with the swarthy complexion and bulging muscles, had picked up his last passenger he turned off the engine of the bus. From his driver's seat he said, "Listen up, kids while I go over my rules with you. Number 1: No cussing. Number 2: No fighting. Number 3: No sassing the driver." Flexing his muscles, he continued in a strong voice: "If you're ready to follow my rules, welcome. If you have trouble following any of my rules, you will no longer have a free ride to school. Have I made myself clear?"

"Yes, sir, Mr. Snyder," they all sang out. "We understand your rules."

Mr. Snyder revved the engine and they resumed their journey. Phyllis, sitting on the front row, clasped her hands together under her chin. The constant humming of the motor made her drowsy. *I wonder what Mama is doing and if Bozo misses me. He seemed so confused when he couldn't come with us.* Phyllis began to nod and before she knew what was happening, she was sound asleep. Only the jolt of the bus stopping and her brother and cousins jostling to exit woke her.

Charles reached over and tapped Phyllis on the shoulder. "This is the end of our ride. Come and I'll introduce you to your teacher. From then on you're on your own. By the way, don't expect to play with me at recess."

"Mrs. Heston," said Charles, "this is my sister, Phyllis. She'll be in your class this year." He turned to Phyllis: "Give Mrs. Heston the note from Daddy."

Mrs. Heston opened the note, read it, and then put it with some other papers in a big zipped-up folder. "Good morning, Phyllis. Welcome to the first grade." The teacher smiled, revealing two dimples, one on either side of her mouth.

Phyllis rolled her baby blue eyes and pushed aside her straggly blond hair and whispered, "Daddy said you'd teach me to read and write."

"Your daddy is absolutely right." Mrs. Heston added, "Phyllis, I trust you'll like school better than your brother Charles. I fear his favorite subjects were recess and lunch."

Phyllis thought to herself, *I hope she doesn't think I'm going to be like Charles. As time passes, she'll find out how eager I am to learn.* Keeping her thoughts to herself, Phyllis dropped her head, too shy to utter a single word.

Mrs. Heston, a stocky built lady in her early 30s, chuckled. "Hmm, I can tell you and I are going to get along fine. Do you like to play baseball?"

Phyllis' eyes lit up and for a brief second she was no longer shy. "Yes, ma'am. Daddy says I've got a good eye for knowing when to swing at a ball."

Soon other children began arriving. Phyllis was assigned to a seat close to the teacher's desk. A girl with two vacant spaces where her front baby teeth once resided was assigned to a desk to the left of Phyllis.

Turning to Phyllis the girl said, "Hi, my name is Bennie. What's your name?"

Phyllis ducked her head and whispered, "I'm Phyllis Edwards."

"Can you jump rope?" asked Bennie. "How about hopscotch?"

Phyllis leaned over and responded, "I'm pretty good at jump roping and hopscotch."

Bennie's eyes danced with mischievousness. "Miss Phyllis, at recess we'll see how good you really are."

Mrs. Heston rang the big bell sitting on her desk, and all talking ceased. Her smile was gone.

"Good morning, class. Welcome to the first grade. We're glad to have you. We'll study hard and when we play, we'll play hard. Listen up as I call the roll."

When Phyllis received her reader, she clutched it to her heart.

Bennie spoke up. "Hugging a book? I don't get it."

Phyllis shrugged her shoulders. "This is my very first book!"

Mom and Aunt Laurie

Homesick Blues

Phyllis had been in school less than a month when she saw the county doctor carrying a small black bag and being ushered into a tiny room near the principal's office.

"Class," said Mrs. Heston, "today each of you will be given a shot to keep you from coming down with a disease that could take your life."

Remembering Charles' vivid description of getting a shot, Phyllis began wringing her hands. Bennie was in line just behind Phyllis. Through the thin walls Phyllis could hear some of the kids crying.

One young fellow walked out of the tiny room, gritting his teeth and bawling up his fist as he declared: "I'd like to snatch Doc Lillard's shooter. I'd show that old crow how it feels to get a shot!"

Phyllis bit her lower lip, determined not to cry.

"Next," called the doctor's nurse.

Phyllis rolled up her shirt sleeve, held out her arm, and closed her eyes. Doc Lillard administered the three-in-one shot. Although Phyllis wanted to cry, she controlled her instincts. Instead, she rubbed her arm and quickly returned to her classroom.

On a Saturday afternoon several months later Phyllis sat bug-eyed on the front porch, totally engrossed in the conversation going on between Mama and Aunt Laurie.

"Did you hear about neighbor Johnson coming down with pneumonia?" asked Aunt Laurie.

"Yes," said Mama. "Did he go see a doctor?"

Aunt Laurie nodded her head. "The doctor said he should be put in the hospital and begin taking penicillin."

"Isn't that the high-powered drug that saved the lives of many American soldiers during World War II?" asked Mama.

"Yes," said Laurie. "Until recently penicillin was very expensive."

Mama slowly shook her head. "If you ask me, it's still too expensive for poor folks. If any of my family gets pneumonia, we'll never come up with enough money for penicillin."

Phyllis grabbed her doll and sped to her attic room. She added her doll to the line of other dolls sitting on her bed. Using a large sewing needle, she proceeded to give each of her dolls a shot. She spoke soothingly to each doll, just like Doctor Lillard did when he gave her an immunization: "Don't tell Mama or Aunt Laurie, but I've got lots of penicillin and it won't cost you a penny." Once she finished administering the shots, Phyllis pulled up the covers until her doll patients seemed comfortable. As she turned to leave, she whispered, "Take a little nap and I'll be back later to check on you."

When Monday morning arrived Phyllis watched as Mama, slower than usual, prepared breakfast. Without a warning, Mama began coughing. "Mama," said Phyllis, "I'm going to stay home and take care of you."

Mama squared her shoulders. "You'll do no such thing. Don't you worry about me. I'll be alright."

Phyllis frowned, picked up her book satchel, and followed Charles to the bus stop. All day during school she kept thinking about Mama's coughing spells and about the conversation Aunt Laurie and Mama had on the front porch. She sat under a tree while her friends played hopscotch at recess, and during lunch she picked at her food.

Upon returning to her classroom, Phyllis began crying. At first it was only little sniffs. Finally, she began sobbing and grabbed the attention of everyone.

Her friends hovered around her, and Mrs. Heston inquired: "Phyllis, what's wrong? Has someone hurt your feelings? Are you sick?"

Phyllis shook her head. "I'm homesick for Mama. She was sick this morning. Mrs. Heston, Mama hasn't ever had one of Doctor Lillard's shots. She might die from some dread disease."

Mrs. Heston scratched her head. "Phyllis, I'm sure your mother is fine, or I would have heard from her. Will it make you feel any better if I let you stay in your brother's classroom until it's time to go home?"

Before Phyllis could answer, Mrs. Heston took her by the hand and deposited her in Charles' classroom. For the next two hours, Phyllis spent her time dodging rubberband assaults by several boys while Charles totally ignored her.

When the dismissal bell rang, Phyllis leaped from her desk and raced for the bus. As soon as the bus stopped at Sheed's Creek, Phyllis made a beeline to find Mama. "How are you, Mama?" she asked.

Mama smiled. "I took a hefty dose of castor oil, and I'm almost as good as new. Did you bring me some books to read?"

Phyllis sighed with relief, "Oh, I'm so glad you don't have pneumonia." Phyllis cupped her hand over her mouth. "Mama, I forgot all about getting you any books. I was so worried about you, I made a spectacle of myself."

Mama laughed. "Well, I appreciate you being so concerned about me, but I don't think a spectacle was necessary."

Phyllis nodded. "I cried and cried. Finally, Mrs. Heston put me in Charles' room to help me feel better. But that didn't work! All the boys shot rubberbands at me and Charles let them. Forgive me, Mama, for not bringing you any books." Phyllis hugged Mama and told her, "I'm so proud of you. I do believe you've read every book I've ever brought home!"

From the time Phyllis was in the first grade, she always had a boyfriend. Her first boyfriend, like Phyllis, was shy, good-looking, and had a great big smile. His name was Jimmy Rose, and she couldn't wait to get home to tell Mama and Aunt Laurie about him.

"Since yesterday was Valentine's Day, Mrs. Heston asked the boys to go sit by their sweethearts. Jimmy twisted and squirmed but remained in his seat. So, I slowly made my way to Jimmy's desk. He smiled and made room for me to sit by him."

Aunt Laurie asked, "What happened then? Did he kiss you?"

Phyllis blushed. "We just sat there smiling at each other. Of course, he didn't kiss me."

Mama beamed with pride. "Phyllis, how did that make you feel?"

Phyllis giggled. "It's kind of nice to know the best-looking fellow in our class is my sweetheart."

The months rolled by and soon school was out for the summer. By the end of Phyllis' first year in school she found herself able to read books that were far above her grade level. Even though it was unheard of, the school librarian let Phyllis choose a stack of books to read over the summer months. On the last day of school, Phyllis happily lugged home books about famous medical discoveries and doctors. She eagerly delved into her library books and afterwards shared them with her mama, who felt stymied because she had to drop out of school in the eighth grade to help at home. Mama loved to read.

A Bigger World

School had been out less than two weeks when Phyllis' friends Bennie and Pam came for a visit. Giving each of them a bear hug, Phyllis yelled: "Mama, Daddy, Charles. Come meet my school friends!"

Mama smiled at the girls. "Phyllis has talked so much about the two of you until I feel like we're old friends."

Daddy tipped his work cap. "You're here just in time to christen our new flying jenny."

Charles had been shyly sneaking a look at Pam from behind his father. He stepped forward, saying, "Let me help you with your overnight bags." Phyllis couldn't believe her ears. *Is this my brother suddenly being Mr. Nice Guy?*

Bozo, wagging his tail and issuing a string of shrill barks, moved in to sniff out the visitors.

Soon Mama called up to Phyllis' attic room. "Dinner will be ready in about two hours. I hope you all like fried chicken and fresh vegetables. How does banana pudding sound for dessert?"

Bennie answered back, "Mrs. Edwards, did you ever hear of a southern gal who didn't like fried chicken? Pam and I love fried chicken, and we can't wait to sample your banana pudding!"

Soon the girls came downstairs and Phyllis took them outside for a brief lay of the land. Bozo trailed behind while Phyllis pointed out the basketball goal her daddy had made and their walking stilts and their newest attraction, the flying jenny.

Pam spoke up. "I've heard of a flying jenny but have never ridden on one. Can we try it out?"

Charles, who was standing nearby with his eyes still fixed on Pam, was quick to speak. "Sure thing! Pam, you and Bennie need to take a seat on either end of the long pole attached to the stump of the tree. To get the two of you swirling around and around, I'll stand behind you, Pam, and push you around. At the same time Phyllis will stand behind Bennie and push her around. Don't either of you get off until the flying jenny comes to a complete stop."

When the ride was over, Pam exclaimed: "Whew! That was some ride. I'm going to talk with my daddy about making a flying jenny for us."

Phyllis dropped her head. "I know both of you at home have electricity, indoor plumbing, and telephones. We don't have any of those conveniences." She pointed toward a dilapidated structure. "If you have to potty, there is where you go."

Quick to change the subject, Bennie said, "Phyllis, when are you coming to visit me?"

Pam chimed in, "And when are you coming to see me?"

Phyllis laughed. "Mama and I have been talking it over. As both of you know, I've never spent the night away from home." She paused. "However, I'm coming soon to see both of you. My Uncle Harle will give me a ride to Ocoee in his pickup truck."

By now they had arrived full circle and standing in the doorway was Phyllis' mama.

"Dinner's ready," she said. "I hope you all are hungry."

Bennie and Pam's eyes grew big as they scanned the table laden with fried chicken, corn on the cob, hot buttered biscuits, fresh sliced tomatoes, and cantaloupes.

Charles passed the platter of fried chicken to Pam, and the feast was underway!

"Save room for some of Mama's banana pudding," warned Phyllis.

After helping herself to two servings of banana pudding, Bennie, rubbing her full stomach, said, "Mrs. Edwards, you're a great cook. I haven't got room for another bite."

Mama's eyes danced with mischief. "Are you really too full? I was thinking that in a couple of hours you girls would be ready for a batch of my chocolate fudge."

Pam flung both of her hands in the air. "Pay no mind to Bennie's talk. The story of your homemade fudge is well known at Ocoee School. Believe me, we'll be ready. The very thought of homemade fudge has my mouth watering."

Bennie and Pam were intrigued with the old building still standing on the Edwards' property. "Can we go inside?" asked Bennie.

"We sure can," said Phyllis. "Charles and I often swing from the rafters."

Soon the girls were having a grand old time climbing up the exposed poles, with Bennie leaping from one rafter to the next and shouting, "Look, me Tarzan. Where's Jane?"

Phyllis, already poised to follow Bennie's feat, got tickled. Soon she was dangling between two rafters, giggling and peeing like crazy.

"Oops!" said Pam. "Sorry, Tarzan. Jane's calling for time out."

To make Phyllis feel better, the three of them exchanged their pee stories as if nothing had happened and then continued playing.

The weekend passed quickly. After her friends left, Phyllis climbed into bed on Sunday night and reflected on their visit. *It doesn't seem to matter to my friends that we don't have modern conveniences.* She was quiet for a second. *What I do have is a mama and a daddy who love me dearly.* Phyllis smiled and soon fell into a deep sleep.

The month of July brought heavy and frequent rains. Even so, the Edwards family members found themselves having unrelenting, hot, muggy days followed by unrelenting, hot, muggy nights.

Phyllis and Mama made plans for Phyllis to spend one week with Bennie and one week with Pam.

Clutching her burlap sack of clothes, Phyllis climbed into the back of Uncle Harle's truck. Sitting close to the tailgate with her legs dangling in midair, Phyllis entertained wild thoughts as to what she would be doing when she got to Bennie's.

When Uncle Harle's truck finally came to a stop, Phyllis hopped down and soon was met with a rousing welcome from Bennie and her two older sisters.

"Welcome, Phyllis," said Bennie's older sister. "We're so glad you've come for a visit. Please make yourself at home."

The other sister chimed in as they entered the living room, "Sometimes around here you have to talk loud to be heard."

Phyllis' eyes fell on the piano in their living room.

"Do you like music?" asked Bennie's older sister. "Maybe you can change Bennie's mind about taking piano lessons. Right now, she's determined to be uncooperative!"

Phyllis' bright blue eyes glistened. "I guess Bennie has other things she finds more interesting." Phyllis let her fingers run over the ivories. "I'd give anything to learn how to play the piano."

Bennie's older sister rubbed her hands together and asked, "Would you like for me to give you a lesson or two about playing the piano?"

Phyllis clutched her hands. "Would you? I'd like that very much."

Bennie tugged on Phyllis' arm. "Come with me and I'll show you where we'll be sleeping, eating, going to the bathroom, taking a bath ... you know, all the necessary things you need to know."

When they got to the bathroom Phyllis' eyes grew big. She asked, "What's that big thing sitting in your bathroom?"

At first Bennie shook her head, puzzled by Phyllis' question. Then she remembered her trip to Phyllis' house. "Oh, we call it a bathtub. You can fill it up with hot or cold water. Before bedtime tonight you can try it out."

The week passed quickly, and soon Phyllis was back home. Her voice was bubbly as she exclaimed: "Mama, something fun to do is always going on at Bennie's house. Everyone made me feel so welcome—even her two brothers. I'll never forget our evening meals together. They have fun being together and made me feel like I was a part of their family."

Mama smiled. "What did you enjoy most about your visit?"

Phyllis paused, cupping her right fist under her chin. "It was a close tie between taking a bath in the big tub and eavesdropping over the party telephone line."

Mama inched forward. "How does a telephone party line work?"

Phyllis rocked to and fro as she talked. "Bennie's family shares a telephone line with six other families. Whenever one of her neighbors gets a telephone call, everyone hears the phone ringing. You know which neighbor is being called by the number of times the phone rings." Phyllis rolled her eyes. "If you want to hear what your neighbor is up to, you carefully pick up the phone and hold your breath while they're talking."

Mama added. "The Lord have mercy!"

Phyllis laughed. "Mama, we listened in every time Pam's phone rang."

Mama's brow wrinkled. "Tell me about the bathtub. Was it fun?"

"It was about five times the size of one of our zinc washtubs. To fill it with water, you put a stopper in a hole and run hot or cold water that comes out of a pipe right in the wall. You don't have to heat the water on the stove or anything." Phyllis' eyes danced with mischief. "I filled it to the brim and pretended I was in a swimming pool."

Mama's eyes grew large. "I do declare! What will they think of doing next?"

"Mama, once I got the hang of it, I stayed so long until Bennie came to check and see if I was alright." Phyllis laughed. "I slid down the back of the tub into the water until my bottom turned red."

That was all it took. Mama and Phyllis doubled over in unrestrained laughter.

Phyllis' next visit was to see Pam. She'd barely arrived when Pam's mother sent a cold chill down Phyllis' spine. "My goodness, child," she said as she stared at Phyllis' stringy blond hair. "Who is your hairdresser?"

Phyllis dropped her head and pushed back her windblown hair. She mumbled, "I guess you can tell I've never had a hair stylist. Mama fills a zinc tub with water from the creek every Saturday and, after my body gets scrubbed, Mama washes my hair." Pam's mother rolled her eyes and Pam whispered, "Your hair's okay with me. Come and I'll get you settled in, and then we can play with my paper dolls."

As Phyllis and Pam headed for Pam's room, Pam's older sister shoved Pam to one side and glared at Phyllis. "You and your friend had better stay clear of my room." She gritted her teeth and her eyes flashed daggers as she entered her bedroom and slammed the door.

Pam confided to Phyllis. "She's an old windbag, but I'm not afraid of her and neither should you let her frighten you."

Phyllis gulped for air. "Pam, let's play paper dolls later on. Instead, let's go outside and climb a tree."

Pam shook her head. "Phyllis, we don't have any trees to climb." She extended her hands. "As you can see, our house lies between a railroad track and a busy highway."

Phyllis clapped her hands. "Well, how about a game of hopscotch?"

"Yes," said Pam. "That sounds like fun."

Around the dinner table that night everyone ate in silence as if conversation was forbidden. The constant scowl Pam's sister wore made Phyllis uneasy, as she thought to herself, *This is so different from eating at Bennie's. At Bennie's the whole room came alive with stories and laughter.*

The next morning Pam and Phyllis were enjoying a game of jackstones when the ball took an unexpected turn and rolled down the hallway. Before they realized it, they were standing at the forbidden door of Pam's mother's in-house beauty shop. Towering over the girls, Pam's mother said sternly, "Get your ball and leave. A beauty shop is no place for children."

Phyllis' problems continued through the hours of the night. Every time she came close to falling asleep, the squeaking brake stops and honking horns of semi-trucks or the forlorn whistle sounds of approaching trains jolted her awake. She sighed as she tossed and turned. *Oh, what I'd give to be home with only the occasional sound of a screech owl to disturb my sleep.*

Before Phyllis knew what was happening, it was time to begin another year of school. As she did in first grade, she excelled in her studies, deepened her friendship with Bennie and Pam, and continued adding new boyfriends to her ever-growing list of male admirers. While Phyllis' self-confidence blossomed academically, she continued to be ill at ease among her more affluent peers. However, when it came to competitions, sports or otherwise, Phyllis always played to win! Whether it was running a race, playing softball, or shooting marbles, she gave the task at hand her best efforts.[1]

Phyllis' early artwork

28

Christmas Joy

Christmas for parents happens faster than melting ice cream on a hot summer day, while for children the days before Christmas move slower than molasses being poured over a hot biscuit. Christmas is a remembering time. It doesn't matter whether you're poor or rich, male or female, young or old, at Christmas we all return home.

One of the Edwards family's most cherished traditions was going to the woods with Daddy in search of a Christmas tree. In early December of Phyllis' third year in school she and Charles accompanied their father on their annual pilgrimage.

"How about this one, Daddy?" asked Charles, pointing to a tall cedar tree. "It has lots of low branches and would be easy to decorate."

Phyllis shook her head. "Daddy, that tree will never do! One of its sides has full branches, but its other side has stubby branches all chunked together."

Charles took another look. "As much as it pains me to admit it, Phyllis, you're right."

With that decision settled, Charles summoned: "Come, Phyllis Ann. We can't stop until we find the right tree."

After an hour of searching, all three of them stopped abruptly in front of a cypress that seemed to say, "Pick me. I'm perfect for the job."

Delighted to have Charles and Phyllis in agreement, Daddy wasted no time cutting the tree down and hauling it back to the house. Soon he mounted the tree on a stand and brought it into the living room. Phyllis watched as Mama retrieved their small box of red Christmas rope, last year's tinsel, and a few ornaments.

It soon became evident that Phyllis and Charles had different ideas on how to go about decorating the tree. Charles took a hand full of tinsel strips and threw the entire wad toward a low-hanging branch, as he exclaimed, "Let's get this decorating over with so we can go outside and play."

"Daddy," whined Phyllis, "come see what Charles calls decorating the tree."

Daddy took one look at the mass of tinsel all on one branch and shook his head. Grinning, he took Charles by the hand and suggested: "Let's leave the decorating to the women folk. I need you to help me cut some holly berries. Who knows? Perhaps we'll find some mistletoe."

Before the hours of night began creeping over their farmstead, the mystical aura of Christmas had transformed their otherwise plain dwelling into a place of beauty and expectancy.

≈

Right after Thanksgiving the women of Cookson Creek Baptist Church began practicing for the annual Christmas pageant. This would be the first year that Phyllis, now almost nine, was old enough to participate in the production.

It was a given that the director's daughter would play the part of Mary and that Wendell, the song leader's eldest son, would be Joseph. There was some discussion on who would play the part of Gabriel. Finally, it was decided that Phyllis Edwards, providing she could speak loudly enough, would be given the role. But for a while it looked as if Phyllis wasn't going to work out as Gabriel.

"Phyllis," said the director, "you must speak so that people on the last row of pews can hear you. Let me hear you say, 'Fear not! Behold! I bring you good tidings of great joy.'"

Phyllis gulped for air and whispered, "Fear not!"

The director gently mocked Phyllis' response. "I could barely hear you—and I'm sitting on the front row. Pretend you're mad at Charles. Phyllis, get louder!"

This went on for what seemed like an eternity until Phyllis felt like she was shouting, "FEAR NOT!"

The director smiled. "Good! You got it right that time."

"But, Mrs. Smith, I was screaming."

"I know and that's what it takes for you to be heard by everyone. Remember you're no longer Phyllis Edwards but a mighty angel with news everyone needs to hear."

As the time for the play drew near, Phyllis practiced her lines on everyone—including those who were willing and even those who were unwilling. She'd been threatened by Charles and parroted by her school friends.

From a discarded white sheet, Mama made Phyllis a white robe with full flowing sleeves. She sewed rows of gold braid around the neck and the sleeves.

As was customary, the pageant was held on the Sunday nearest to Christmas Day. Kinfolk from all around had come for the presentation. For this special occasion everyone was decked out in their finest clothing, which for some people meant freshly laundered overalls and red suspenders. Many of the fellows wore air-dried white shirts and a tie. The women and girls arrived wearing simple handmade cotton frocks and some type of hat.

Pastor Allie welcomed the crowd, the song leader signaled to the piano player, and the crowd began singing Christmas carols. The pageant was next on the program.

Mama beamed with pride. She whispered to Arthur, "Isn't Phyllis beautiful?"

Charles, overhearing his mama's comment, whispered back, "She may look like an angel but when she comes at you with her fist clenched, even we fellows know to duck."

The pageant proceeded without a bobble. Gabriel appeared before a group of trembling ragtag shepherds and urged them not to be afraid but to find the baby nestled in a stable.

Once the pageant was over, Phyllis, still in her angel's robe, made a beeline for Daddy's old 1940 Chevrolet. When Mama asked her why she left without letting everyone tell her how well she played the role of Gabriel, she grinned and replied, "I don't enjoy having a bunch of people making a fuss over me. Mama, I'm just glad it's over! Can we go home?"

Phyllis had her heart set on getting a bride doll for Christmas. She made sure everyone knew what was on her wish list.

Dear Santa,

I've made good grades at school and go to church most every Sunday. Would you please bring me a bride doll? You can find the one I want in the department store in Cleveland. I hope you and your reindeer don't have any trouble finding our house. My brother Charles and I will be looking for you on Christmas Eve.

Love,
Phyllis

Just in case some of the rumors about there not being a real Santa Claus were true, Phyllis also made sure Mama and Daddy knew what she wanted.

On Christmas morning Phyllis flew down the stairs and made her way to the Christmas tree. Suddenly her face fell 10 feet. Under the tree with her name on it was a beautiful doll. "Oh," she said, "There must be some mistake. I asked Santa for a bride doll." Nevertheless, she picked up her gift doll and tried to look happy. But while Phyllis was perplexed, Mama's eyes were dancing: she seemed so happy. Phyllis withdrew from the family fun to enjoy her self-pity.

"Phyllis, don't give up so quickly," said Mama. "Keep looking. You might find another doll."

Phyllis returned and began combing every angle of the tree until way back in a lonely spot she found her bride doll. She grabbed the doll in her arms and ran to hug Mama and Daddy.

"Mama, look what I found! You must have known where Santa hid my bride doll. Oh, I'm so very happy!"

"Phyllis," said Mama, "The first doll is one of the dolls you've been giving shots. I repaired Patricia's arm and made her a new outfit. Isn't she beautiful?"

"Mama, forgive me. You did such a good job repairing and dressing Patricia that I didn't recognize her."

Phyllis, with both dolls in tow, turned to go to her room when she heard Daddy say, "It's time we leave for our Christmas visit to Harle's. I'm going outside to get the car started. I'll honk on the horn when I get it going."

"Children, put on your heavy coats," said Mama. "It's liable to be snowing before we get back home."

In a few weeks even the magic of Christmas gifts began to wane and it was time to bundle up and return to school.

The Importance of Education

It was late September and Phyllis, now nine, had been in the fourth grade less than two weeks when a drenching rain accompanied by howling winds began falling all over Polk County. The rivers, lakes, and creeks reached treacherous levels. The land bridge across Sheeds Creek washed away, posing a transportation hazard.

Wearing a heavy frown, Phyllis lamented, "Daddy, how will I get to school tomorrow?"

"Phyllis, don't you worry about that," assured Daddy. "I'll get you to school. My Mama used to say, 'When there is a will, a way will be made.'"

Phyllis crunched her shoulders and asked with puzzlement, "Are we going to swim across the creek?"

Her daddy chuckled. "There will be no swimming. I'll carry you over on Tarzan. After I get you to the school loading zone I'll come back and get Charles."

Charles made an ugly face. "Why don't you carry Miss Phyllis Ann across and leave me here?"

Grinning, Daddy said, "You'd like that, wouldn't you, Charles? Rest assured I'm taking you across the creek."

Throughout the night and into the morning strong rains continued to ravage the already soaked land. Daddy arrived with Tarzan and Phyllis hopped on the horse, clasping her arms around Daddy's waist. Turning her head back toward the house, Phyllis saw Mama standing in the doorway wringing her hands.

Just then Tarzan stumbled and swayed as he tried to keep his footing in the swift waters. As Phyllis watched her daddy struggle to stay above the water line, she thought, *Mama is worried, but not me. My daddy is brave and strong, and so is Tarzan. The two of them will get me safely across this creek. I'm sure of that!*

Quick! Get a Doctor

Ocoee School officials were struggling to manage the effects of the bad weather sweeping their area when shocking family news invaded the Edwards household.

Phyllis could always tell when Mama was upset. Mama would walk the floor, wringing her hands—just as she was doing right now. "Charles, make a beeline to Uncle Harle's," she called. "Tell him your daddy is very sick and that your mama wants him to fetch Doctor Lillard."

Charles left at once.

Phyllis squeezed Mama's hands and tried to comfort her. "Mama, don't worry. Maybe Daddy has a nasty cold."

Mama shook her head. "I fear it's much worse than a cold. Daddy's fever is high and he's having spells where he breaks out sweating, and then in a few minutes he's shaking like a leaf. I tried putting several blankets over him." Mama started crying. "The blankets didn't help. He's still shaking, and he's having trouble breathing."

Phyllis hurried to Daddy's room. She took note that he'd peeled back the extra quilts and was struggling to get his breath. She handed him a glass of water. "Daddy, drink this. It will bring your fever down."

Daddy was listless and Phyllis, not knowing what else to do, sat in the chair near where Daddy lay and continuously wiped his forehead with a damp cloth.

Charles returned in about an hour with the news that Uncle Harle left immediately for Benton to get Doctor Lillard. Meanwhile, Phyllis kept her eye on the wind-up tabletop clock in the living room as the minutes turned into hours. Mama continued walking the floor and wringing her hands.

"With all of the storms we've had, there's no telling what kind of shape the roads are in," said Charles.

When Phyllis returned from Daddy's room she said, "Mama, Daddy is having another chilling spell. I heaped all the blankets back on him." She began to cry. "It breaks my heart to see Daddy shaking. I do hope Dr. Lillard gets here soon."

Everyone was on edge with worry when there came a heavy rapping on the front door and someone said, "Open the door and let us in!"

Charles barged to the door. "I'd know that voice anywhere. That's Uncle Harle." Swinging open the door, Charles urged, "Do come in."

"The land crossings across the creeks have all washed away," said Uncle Harle. "We had to walk the last mile to get here."

Phyllis took their soaked raincoats as Mama said, "I knew something unforeseen had happened. Can I fix the two of you a cup of coffee?"

Doctor Lillard smiled. "I'd like that very much, Mrs. Edwards. Meantime, take me to my patient."

Charles and Phyllis followed the doctor into the room where Daddy lay in his sick bed. They watched as Doctor Lillard checked out Daddy's vital signs. "It's just as I thought," he said. "Arthur has pneumonia. I'll give him a shot of penicillin." Then, in a half-serious, half-teasing voice, he added: "Would the two of you like to have a shot of penicillin?"

Phyllis and Charles, remembering all too well their vaccination shots at school, had heard more than they wanted to hear. Both of them made a mad dash to get out of the room. After they had gained a little distance, Phyllis whispered to Charles: "Let's hide in the closet. No one will find us there."

Doctor Lillard methodically gave Daddy a shot of penicillin. When he'd finished, he asked, "Is there anyone here who can give Mr. Edwards a shot for a few days?"

Mama grew pale and looked as if she were going to faint. Uncle Harle laughed as he faced the doctor. "Where did everyone go? That leaves only me. Doctor Lillard, I'll see that Arthur gets his shots."

After prompting Uncle Harle on how to give the penicillin shots, the doctor lingered long enough to drink a cup of coffee and to give Phyllis' mama some pointers on how to take care of her husband.

Doctor Lillard said to Harle, "Stay here with your kinfolk. I won't have any trouble finding my way back to Benton."

Four hours passed and it was time for Daddy to get his second penicillin shot. Phyllis watched every move Uncle Harle made when he gave Daddy his second shot. "Mama, Daddy's sitting up and hasn't had a chilling spell in hours. It's no wonder they call penicillin a miracle drug."

After dispensing the shot, Uncle Harle turned to dispose of the needle. Phyllis said, "Uncle Harle, can I have that empty shot container?"

Uncle Harle threw up his hands. "I don't know what you can do with it, but go ahead and help yourself."

With her empty penicillin shooter in hand, Phyllis rushed to her bedroom. There she lined up her dolls and gave each of them a shot. For as long as Daddy was recovering, she inoculated her dolls. So vigorously did she administer shots to them, their sawdust innards began dribbling to the floor.

The Pianist

Phyllis yearned to become a pianist. Long before she entered the first grade, she dreamed of owning and playing a piano. She even made a piano out of a cardboard box, complete with piano keys.

"Look, Mama," she said, "I'm playing the piano just like our church pianist. Aren't you proud of me?"

Now that she was in the fourth grade, Phyllis harassed her parents every day to get her a piano.

"Arthur," said Mama, "Phyllis Ann wants a piano so she can practice here at home. Can't you come up with some way we can get her one?"

Phyllis' daddy sat for a long while in deep thought. Finally, he clapped his hands together. "Here's what we'll do. I'll buy Phyllis a pig. If she looks after and feeds the pig every day, when the pig is big enough to be sold, she can have all the money the pig brings for her piano."

"That sounds reasonable to me," said Mama. "Phyllis, what do you think of Daddy's plan?"

Phyllis danced a little jig. "Daddy," she said, "come rain or shine, the bitter cold of winter or the sweltering heat of summer, I'll carry slop twice every day to feed my pig. I promise you won't have to remind me a single time."

Meanwhile, the days turned into weeks and the weeks turned into months.

Phyllis kept her word and every day until the pig became a hog, she carried a bucket of slop twice a day up a steep hill to the pigpen. Daddy also kept his word. By the end of Phyllis' fourth grade in school, she had a piano.

Daddy covered his ears as Phyllis continuously hit the wrong notes while practicing. He teased Phyllis' mama, "Tell me, Lela, will our Phyllis ever get to where she can play an entire song without messing up?"

Mama smiled. "You know our daughter. She'll never stop until she gets it right. In the meantime, we might need to put a little cotton in our ears."

Daddy shook his head. "When Phyllis sets her mind to do something, sooner or later it's going to be done. Honey, can you find me a wad of cotton?"

By the fourth grade, Wendell Price took over as Phyllis' beau. He supplied her with a nickel every day for ice cream. When Phyllis told Mama about that, Mama punched her sister Laurie in the ribs and commented. "Now that's what I call a good one. If Wendell's daddy knew his son was buying ice cream for Arthur Edwards' child, he'd throw a hissy fit."

Sunday Go-to-Meeting Days

Going to church most Sundays was a regular part of family life in the Edwards household. Only the worst of weather conditions or their defunct Chevrolet hindered them from attending.

On one particular Saturday, Mama, with Phyllis trailing behind her, hustled around the house and laid out certain clothes to be worn the following day. She turned to Phyllis and warned, "How many times do I have to tell you that you can't wear your jeans to church?"

"But Mama, why can't I? Does God not like blue jeans?"

Mama, trying to mask her frustration, stared at Phyllis and said nothing.

Phyllis grabbed Mama's arm. "Why can Charles wear blue jeans to church but not me? Why, Mama? Why?"

"I reckon," said Mama, "It's because Charles would look a little silly wearing a dress."

Imagining Charles wearing a dress set off Phyllis' tickle box.

"Okay, Mama, you win and I lose!"

Once the Edwards family arrived at Cookson Creek Baptist Church, Phyllis, decked out in a fresh homespun dress, squeezed into the family pew between her parents. After about 30 minutes of rousing gospel singing, Pastor Allie Hall strode to the pulpit.

Holding his oversized King James Bible in clear view of everyone, he began ranting and raving as he bobbled and weaved across the tiny stage area. Sweat poured down his face. The armpits of his homespun blue shirt were soaked. Phyllis flinched as the preacher's strident voice denounced sinners bound for an endless hell. She could feel the devil waiting, eager to devour her.

After they got home Phyllis inquired, "Mama, why does Pastor Allie get so angry when he's preaching?"

Mama smiled. "He's not angry. He just wants people to understand what it will be like if they don't repent of their sins."

Charles entered the conversation. "Can someone tell me why the same two men come to the altar weeping and carrying on every Sunday?"

Phyllis' eyes sparkled with interest as Daddy answered. "The two of them spend Saturday nights at the local honkytonk in Benton guzzling down liquor." He grinned and added, "I guess they hope God has a short memory."

Phyllis found it fascinating to watch the stream of people moving toward the altar at church. One Sunday a rotund woman in her late 50s, with her face set in stone, approached the altar accompanied by her reluctant husband. The couple lingered at the rail of the altar in serious conversation with the pastor. Finally, they stood up. Phyllis heard the woman tell her husband: "I'll forgive you this time, but if you ever go gallivanting off with another woman one more time, you'll be sorry!"

In addition to preaching and confessing, gospel music was the soul food that knit the congregation of Cookson Baptist together. Phyllis was no exception: she loved the gospel hymns.

For weeks on end in late April the Edwards family and their neighbors far and near began preparing for homecoming at Cookson Creek Baptist Church. For that little clan of believers, this was the biggest social event of the year.

Phyllis' mouth watered as she anticipated sinking her teeth into fried chicken, corn on the cob, vine-ripened tomatoes, Mama's banana pudding, and her Aunt Noonie's caramel cake.

At last the big day arrived. Phyllis' daddy and her brother Charles transported the kitchen goodies in a large wooden crate to the trunk of their 1940 Chevrolet. Phyllis, decked out in a soft pink dress with an embroidered collar, crawled in the back seat of the car along with Mama.

Daddy said, "Lela, say a little prayer that we'll make it to Cookson Creek Baptist Church and back home without losing our brakes or having a flat tire."

Around 10:00 a.m. they arrived at the church. Several of Phyllis' cousins rushed to greet them. Her cousin Don bowed to Phyllis, saying, "You're looking mighty pretty today. Who's your latest sweetheart, and is it true you're going to play the piano today?"

Phyllis blushed. "Which of my latest sweethearts do you want to hear about?" And without waiting for him to respond, she added: "I now have a piano at home and I can play 'I'll Fly Away' and 'What a Friend We Have in Jesus.' I also am taking piano lessons at school."

Once inside the church, Phyllis sat in the pew occupied by Mama and Daddy while Charles finagled a way to sit with the older boys. Reverend Allie was wearing a white, long-sleeved shirt and a blue necktie. The musicians arrived with their banjos, mouth harps, guitars, autoharps, and tambourines. One fellow even had an accordion.

The singing commenced and Phyllis clapped her hands to the lively music and joined in the singing. After an hour of singing, the preacher gave a rousing welcome to the house full of people. There was no altar call this day. Sinners would have to put a hold on their confessions until another Sunday rolled around!

For once, Brother Allie didn't rant and rave. Phyllis heard someone whisper, "The sooner he hushes, the quicker we can get to the fried chicken." Before the preacher could catch his wind and get started on his second sermon, one of the deacons tugged on Pastor Allie's arm and told him, "Reverend, remind them of the afternoon sing festival and then lead us in thanking God for our food."

Pastor Allie bit his lower lip and did as he was told. Soon the people began milling toward the hastily constructed long table groaning with food fit for a king.

No one was prepared for what happened next. A four-legged creature leaped from a nearby cluster of bushes and with the speed of lightning grabbed Aunt Ione's prized ham shank and bolted toward the nearby woods. Soon only the white tip of his waving tail was in full view. Phyllis heard her aunt yell. "Don Edwards, get yourself over here! That thieving beagle of yours has stolen our shank of ham."

Don shook his head in disbelief. "I don't get it! I penned Butch up before we left." He motioned to his buddies. "Help me corral Butch. He's liable to be back for seconds if we don't stop him dead in his tracks."

The boys, leaving behind a small whirlwind of dust, charged toward the deep woods. Caught up in the excitement, Phyllis, all decked out in her new Sunday go-to-meeting dress, took off after them yelling, "Wait for me!"

Running lickety-split through the woods, Phyllis soon became entwined in a thorny bush. She glanced down at her new dress that was now in shreds. *Mama will never forgive me. My dress is ruined, and I have yet to play the piano.* She rubbed her hands together and yanked herself free. It wasn't long until she came upon the group of boys staring at Butch—who was baring his teeth and daring them to come between him and his ham bone.

Charles sneered at Phyllis. "Won't you ever learn you can't do the things we fellows do?" He giggled. "Mama's going to pitch a hissy fit when she sees what you've done to your new dress."

Phyllis said nothing. Instead she snapped off a twig from a nearby tree and yelled, "Here, Butch. Here, Butch! Fetch the stick."

Suddenly Butch darted for the stick, retrieved it, and laid it at Phyllis' feet. Meanwhile, the boys lassoed Butch and carried him back to the crime scene. To make sure Butch didn't escape again, Don and his friends took turns dog-watching.

When Mama saw Phyllis, she shook her head. "The Lord have mercy! I can't believe you joined in with the fellows to chase Don's beagle." She paused before continuing and with a tiny smile adding, "Princess, look at your dress. It's ruined and you're scheduled to play the piano in less than an hour. My, my, my Phyllis Ann. I don't know what I'm going to do with you!"

Phyllis hugged Mama. "Please forgive me. All I could think of was Butch devouring Aunt Ione's ham shank. Somebody had to catch him!"

Mama returned Phyllis' hug. "Now, now, Princess. Don't you cry. Hurry up and eat a bite, and then I'll see what I can do to get you presentable before you play the piano."

By the time it was Phyllis' turn to play two hymns, the news of her wild goose chase to bring Butch to justice was known by everyone. After her presentation in her tattered new dress, the crowd gave Phyllis a huge round of applause. The official song leader said, "Cookson Creek has a new piano player. Thank you, Miss Phyllis!"

Relieved, Mama sighed heavily and was overheard to remark, "This is one church homecoming I'll never forget!"

However, this was not the end of their homecoming day woes. The Edwards family was two miles from home and had just crossed a small creek when a series of repeated thundering noises shattered the air.

Daddy turned and faced his family. "It seems all our tires chose this exact moment to die." He motioned with his hands. "What else can I say? Everyone, climb out. We'll have to hoof it the rest of the way home. Tomorrow I'll see about getting us some new tires."

As they walked arm-in-arm down the lane toward home, Phyllis Ann began singing "I'll Fly Away." Soon everyone joined in. When at last the Edwards straggled up the porch of their farmstead, they barely made it inside the front door before they all fell to the floor and in seconds were sound asleep. There they remained until it was well past noon the following day.

Making Choices

Teachers were very important to Phyllis. Among her favorites was her fourth-grade teacher, Mrs. Crouch, who was strict but kind. Phyllis made topnotch progress under Mrs. Crouch, who relied heavily on teaching phonics to help her students with their reading. While Phyllis was an apt student in all of her school subjects, her love of math and science took top billing.

The public schools in Polk County had no access to classroom television sets. This did not deter the innovative Mrs. Crouch, however. Living within a stone's throw of her classroom, she invited her pupils to her home to see on television a significant step in America's space exploration efforts. Her words to her students, "Children, today you are witnessing before your very eyes history being made," made a lasting impression on Phyllis.

Although Phyllis was fond of Mrs. Crouch, she found her handling of one incident at first to be a bit unnerving. After having to momentarily leave the classroom, Mrs. Crouch returned to find blackboard erasers strewn all over the room. Her face grew red as she rapped with her ruler on her desk. "Class," she demanded, "tell me who threw the erasers!"

The deathly silence that followed only served to raise Mrs. Crouch's ire. "If no one is going to tell me who is responsible for this mess, then you leave me with only one option—and that is to punish everyone."

Wringing her hands while biting her lower lip to keep from crying, Phyllis sidled up to Bennie and whispered, "Do you think Mrs. Crouch will spank all of us?"

That's when Bennie broke the silence. "Mrs. Crouch, I threw an eraser and so did a lot of others."

Upon hearing Bennie's confession Mrs. Crouch threw her hands into the air. "At first I thought I'd entered a war zone. I hope all you eraser-throwers had fun!"

Suddenly Mrs. Crouch began laughing, and then the entire class started laughing. After a few minutes she called the class to order. "Against my better judgment I'm going to forget this ever happened, provided you'll all join in cleaning up your mess."

Phyllis, along with everyone else, scampered to retrieve the eraser missiles while trying to rid the room of its dusty aroma.[2]

Hallelujah! I'm Saved

The driving religious force in Phyllis' family was Mama. Cookson Creek Baptist Church was the church Mama had known since she was a child. As Phyllis reached her preteens, she began giving more attention to her final destination in life. According to her pastor, you were either on your way to heaven or destined to burn forever and forever in a fiery hell.

In mid-August just before Phyllis entered the fifth grade, Cookson Creek Baptist Church had what Baptists call a revival—an outright attempt to rescue sinners from the jaws of hell. The visiting evangelist pleaded, "If you are here tonight and you've never been saved, would you please raise your hand?"

Phyllis glanced to her right and then to her left before meekly raising her hand. In a moment the preacher grabbed her hand.

"Come with me to the mourner's bench. Some Christians are waiting to pray with you until you're saved. You don't want to go to hell, do you, little girl?"

Phyllis shook her head and sank to her knees, then was immediately surrounded by church members with good intentions.

Then the evangelist grabbed the next youngster who had raised his hand and followed the same ritual he had followed with Phyllis. This pattern was repeated over and over. Soon there were more sinners at the mourner's bench than there were saints sitting in the roughly constructed pews.

Phyllis thought, *We could be here all night if I don't do something. The sooner I tell them I'm saved, the sooner we can go home.*

Phyllis scrambled to her feet and announced to all those present, "I'm saved."

"Glory! Hallelujah!" shouted the preacher. "Brother Price, lead us in singing another round of 'Just as I Am.'"

Before going to sleep that night, Phyllis prayed: *Lord, I hope you'll forgive me for telling those people I was saved. I know and you know I'm still not saved. Our revival preacher embarrassed me. I may be wrong, but I feel like the only thing he was interested in was in the number of people making confessions. Lord, he didn't even know my name.*

Teens
1960-1965

Phyllis' 8th-grade class

Teenagers Will Be Teenagers

Although Cookson Creek Baptist Church was Phyllis' home church, during her teen years she preferred going to Shiloh Baptist, located in Ocoee and near where Bennie and Pam lived.

Phyllis relished the social aspects of church. The back row of the church sanctuary was the gathering spot for Phyllis and her teenage friends. To masquerade their social activities, they went into action as soon as someone in the congregation was called to lead in prayer.

As quickly as the people bowed their heads, the teenagers began swapping pictures of their latest beaus and exchanging scribbled notes. The young people were primed to stop immediately when the person praying said the familiar words, "In Jesus' name I pray, Amen." At that point the teenagers dutifully bowed their heads and opened their eyes with the rest of the congregation.

Mischievous plans are known to have flaws, however, and their little scheme was no exception. One of the ushers had, unknowingly to the teenagers, been observing their innocent yet somewhat irreverent behavior.

Motioning to the two rows of teenagers who were busy exchanging their treasured photos, he summoned, "Come, with me. I have just the place for you." He proceeded to lead them down the right center aisle to the front row of pews.

Phyllis whispered to Bennie, "I hope this doesn't get back to Mama. She'd be terribly embarrassed to know I've been cutting up during church."

"With no telephone in your home you're safe," said Bennie. "But mine and Pam's parents are in the congregation today, so we won't be so lucky."

It so happened that one of the high school teachers, Mrs. Poston, occupied a place in the pew behind the teenagers. Mrs. Poston loved to sing, so she belted out her off-key version of the hymns with gusto. The more the teenagers tried to mask their amusement at her singing, the harder the task became.

It started with smiles, followed by soft giggles. Phyllis closed her eyes and desperately tried to control her tickle box. Before she knew what was happening, though, all of the teenagers were caught up in a spasm of uncontrolled laughter. Even the pews housing the teenagers rocked with glee. Finally, their laughter became so contagious that the entire congregation became involved, including Mrs. Poston.

Meanwhile, Ocoee Elementary was trying to find solutions to its bulging school population. Phyllis and Bennie rehashed the overcrowded situation. "I don't like split classes, but sometimes they can be a godsend," said Phyllis. Bennie snickered, "I take it you aren't excited about being in Principal McCamy's class."

Phyllis shuddered. "Bennie, that woman frightens me even when I pass her in the hall. I don't think she believes in laughing. With her it's work, work, work."

Bennie made a shifting sign with her hands. "And if you misbehave, you're shifted to her office faster than you can bat an eye."

"That settles it," said Phyllis. "We'll sign up for Mr. Rice's class. There isn't any sense in making ourselves miserable for an entire year." She paused before adding, "After all, whether we like it or not, we'll all be in Miss McCamy's class next year."

Bennie made an ugly face. "Someone told me that when Miss McCamy learned that you signed up for Mr. Rice's class, she said, 'I don't know what Arthur Edwards has against me that he wants his daughter in another class.'"

Phyllis had just become her school's spelling bee champion when her eighth-grade teacher, Miss Herlein McCamy, approached her saying, "Phyllis, how would you like to be known as the best speller in the state of Tennessee?"

"I'd like that very much," responded Phyllis. "Miss McCamy, do you think I have a ghost of a chance at winning?"

Miss McCamy ran her hands through her closely cropped hair and reset her glasses. "We'll never know unless we try, will we?" She paused, tapping her fingers on her desk. "I'll make a deal with you. Every day I'll give up my teacher break time to help you prepare for the county spelling bee, provided you give up your recess."

Phyllis didn't have to think twice. "I'll give up my recesses, Miss McCamy. When do we start practicing?"

"There's no time like the present," said Miss McCamy. Meet me in my office at 10:30 this morning."

"When is the regional spelling bee?" asked Phyllis, "and where will it be held?"

"It's three months from today and if you win the county spelling bee, you'll represent our county in Knoxville at the University of Tennessee. Do you suppose your daddy could drill you every night at home?"

"Daddy's mother was a teacher," said Phyllis. "I'm sure he'll help me. Daddy loves to help me with my studies."

"Good," said Miss McCamy. "I'll give you a copy of our official spelling list that he can use."

When it was time for recess, Phyllis explained to Bennie and Pam where she would be for the next three months.

Bennie stomped her foot. "Gee whiz, Phyllis, aren't you ever going to get enough school awards?"

Pam let go of a long, low sigh. "Now that you'll be tied up with Miss Stone Face McCamy every day, who's going to teach Bennie and me the facts of life?"

Bennie shrugged her shoulders. "Before you began sharing stuff from your mama's *Home Medical Guide* book, I had a jillion questions—but no answers."

Pam was nodding her head faster than a spinning windmill. "It's the same with me," she said before adding, "You know how it is. No one talks about sex to us—not our parents, our teachers, or our preachers."

Phyllis kept her eyes on her two friends and gently said, "Our discussions also mean a lot to me. After all, I'm learning along with you. After the county spelling bee is over, I promise you we'll resume our talks under the old oak tree."

For the next three months under the watchful eyes of Miss McCamy and Arthur Edwards, Phyllis was never far away from her approved contest spelling rules.

The regional meet was held in Knoxville some 92 miles from Ocoee. Miss McCamy drove Phyllis to Knoxville, leaving Ocoee at 7:30 a.m.

Upon arriving at the University of Tennessee campus, the two of them were led to a huge auditorium rapidly filling up with students and adults. Phyllis was a second away from having a panic attack. She began twisting her hands. "Miss McCamy," she whispered, "what's that thing in front of where I'm to stand?"

Miss McCamy whispered to Phyllis, "It's called a microphone, and its job is to project your voice so the spelling checkers and people in the audience can hear your answers."

Phyllis' eyes grew large, and her voice betrayed her fears. "I've never seen a microphone before, much less had to use one!"

Soon the moderator declared the Tennessee Regional Spelling Bee Contest was officially starting. In less than five minutes the moderator announced, "Phyllis Edwards, your word is balloon."

Phyllis repeated the word balloon. The sound of her name echoing from the microphone was unnerving. She glanced toward the audience and made eye contact with Miss McCamy, who was wearing her continual scowl and seated on the front row with her shoulders stooped. Suddenly Phyllis' mind froze.

Sensing her fright, the moderator repeated: "Phyllis, spell balloon."

My mind is playing dirty tricks on me. Does balloon have two o's and two l's or only one l or one o?

"Balloon," repeated Phyllis, "b-a-l-o-o-n."

"No, I'm sorry, Phyllis; that is incorrect."

Phyllis, while distraught over missing the spelling of balloon, was nevertheless overjoyed she no longer had to speak into that monster they called a microphone. She ducked her head and slowly moved to the side exit behind the stage. Meanwhile, the moderator methodically called on the next contestant, who spelled balloon without any trouble.

Phyllis dreaded driving back to Benton with Miss McCamy. "Phyllis," said Miss McCamy, "I don't understand. I'm certain you know how to spell balloon."

Phyllis burst into tears. "I'm so embarrassed, Miss McCamy. I wasn't on the stage five minutes before I missed the very first word they gave me to spell! I've let you and my school down."

Phyllis at that moment got a view of Miss McCamy's softer side. "Here," she said as she handed Phyllis a tissue. "I'm to blame for not warning you about the microphones and for not telling you we'd have a large crowd of visitors." However, Miss McCamy's softer side went into hiding when they returned to school the following day.

Miss McCamy seemed to be working overtime to expose those students passing notes during class time. She retrieved a note from Bennie addressed to Fred Ezell. Wearing her ever-present scowl, the teacher tore open the note and read aloud: "Dear Fred, Phyllis would like for you to kiss her at recess. Will you?" The note was signed "Bennie."

Phyllis, horrified at being exposed, covered her mouth with her hands and slunk way down in her seat. Meanwhile, the rest of the class enjoyed seeing the school's star pupil squirm.

Phyllis Takes Control

Doctor Smith told the Edwards family that Daddy was a very sick man. "His heart is not functioning well, and he'll need someone to give him a shot every day."

Phyllis watched as Mama's face turned white. "I could never give him a shot," said Mama. She squeezed her hands together. "Doctor Smith, I faint at the sight of blood."

Phyllis stepped forward. "Doctor Smith, if you'll show me how, I'll be glad to give Daddy his shots."

Doctor Smith smiled. "Good for you, Phyllis. We'll start teaching you right away." His nurse brought in an orange and began showing Phyllis how to give a shot. After several good tries on the orange, Phyllis felt competent to give Daddy his shots once they were back home from the doctor's office.

As soon as they returned home, Phyllis designed a chart specifically for Daddy. The chart listed his pulse rate, the time of his shot, and any negative or positive reactions he had to the shot administered.

As the weeks evolved into months, Phyllis carried her report on Daddy to Doctor Smith. "Phyllis, I'm proud of you. Your record-keeping is remarkable. Have you ever given any thought of someday entering the field of medicine?"

Phyllis thought, *Do I dare tell him that night and day I dream about becoming a doctor?* Instead of sharing her thoughts, she said, "That sounds interesting. I believe I'll give it some thought."

"I find it refreshing to find someone in their teens devoted to taking care of their daddy's health," said Doctor Smith. "Have you always been this way?"

Phyllis blushed and slightly shrugged her shoulders. "I guess the good Lord gave me a loving heart for people who are hurting and a willingness to do whatever it takes to make them better."

Phyllis' parents, like most of her neighbors and kinfolk, worried about being able to pay for prescriptions and hospital care. When Phyllis complained of having headaches and waking up tired, it shocked her Mama into action. "Arthur," she said, "We need to take Phyllis to the doctor. Something is wrong with her. She complains of having headaches and wakes up tired. I've been reading in my *Home Medical Guide*, and I'm afraid Phyllis might have leukemia."

Daddy agreed that it wasn't like Phyllis to mope around, so he took her to the doctor. When the doctor diagnosed Phyllis with anemia and prescribed her iron pills, her daddy couldn't resist saying, "Instead of buying iron pills, why couldn't we put a rusty nail in a glass of water and have her drink it? Seems to me it would probably do her as much good as the doctor's pills and—in the meantime—it would save us a little money."

On one occasion when she returned from an appointment with her daddy at Doctor Smith's office, Phyllis went over with her mother the details of her visit. "Mama, the doctor says Daddy's condition is staying about the same and that's a good sign." She lingered near where Mama was mixing the batter for a pound cake.

"Phyllis," asked Mama, "Do you have something else to tell me?"

In a half-whisper Phyllis said, "Mama, I want to be a doctor when I grow up."

Mama pressed her hands against her cheeks. "You have got to be kidding. My little princess a doctor?" She shook her head, trying to absorb what she had just heard. "I hope you change your mind. Becoming a doctor will require you to go to college and, as you know, that costs lots of money. Besides, whoever heard of Polk County having a woman doctor?"

"Mama," begged Phyllis, "Can we keep this conversation just between us? Right now, I know it's an impossible dream." She reached over and hugged Mama. "Dreams, Mama . . . dreams are free!"

In the tenth grade Phyllis had a crush on Don Frady. Every time they passed in the hallway between classes, she felt like her heart would explode. It seemed that everyone except Don knew of her infatuation.

One evening after school was over for the day, Phyllis talked with Bennie. "Since I'm this year's Valentine's queen, do you think it would be alright for me to ask Don to be my escort?"

"Go for it, Phyllis!" encouraged Bennie.

"But what if he turns me down? That would be humiliating."

"Look at it this way," responded Bennie. "The worst thing that could happen would be he's already committed to take someone else."

Phyllis' eyes glistened as she agreed. "Bennie, you're right! I'm going to ask Don to be my escort. Who knows? If I get lucky, I might have a date with the most handsome fellow in school."

When Don said yes, Phyllis was beside herself with joy and set about making her final plans for the big event that was one week away. Everything was lining up well until she stopped by the school office to pick up a copy of the Valentine's dance brochure. Phyllis rolled her eyes and shouted aloud, "Oh, no!" She raced to find Bennie and flung the brochure in Bennie's face. "This can't be! The committee expects Don and me to lead off the entire school with a dance." She moaned. "Bennie, what can I do?" She ran her fingers through her blond hair. "You know I have two left feet. What will Don think of me?"

"All you can do is to go out there and fake it," said Bennie. She laughed. "Let's hope Don's dancing talents exceed yours."

As she imagined the scene where both she and Don were at the mercies of their adoring crowd, Phyllis couldn't help but laugh.

Bennie tapped Phyllis on the shoulder. "Watch me and I'll give you a five-minute dance lesson. Pretend I'm Don. He'll place his arm around your waist and you'll put your right arm on his left shoulder. When he takes a quick step forward with his left foot you take a quick step backwards with your right foot. The steps are quick, quick, slow, slow. Remember he leads and you follow!"

After a few minutes Phyllis' jitters lessened. Every day at recess she practiced with Bennie.

The days passed swiftly and finally the time of the big event was eminent. Don pinned a beautiful corsage on Phyllis' bright red dress. Pods of students were scattered throughout the gymnasium, tapping their feet to the music emanating from the loud speaker. The teacher in charge of the event made a few opening remarks and signaled for the dance to begin.

Don Frady, relaxed and confident, placed his right hand on Phyllis' shoulder.

Phyllis reacted as a frozen zombie. Her face became contorted. Her eyes seemed to beg, "What do we do now?" *Oh gracious me! Don Frady now knows I don't know how to dance. What a predicament!*

Don whispered, "Put your arm around my waist and begin sliding your feet toward me."

Phyllis drew a sigh of relief and attempted to slide her feet forward. However, their feet soon became entangled and the heel of Phyllis' right shoe became disengaged. When she stooped to retrieve it, she stumbled to the floor.

The more experienced dancers, recognizing the dilemma, began dipping their partners. Phyllis, following their lead, took off her high heels and continued to dance in her stocking feet.

Finally, the opening dance number was over. "Phyllis," said Don, "I'm so sorry. This is all my fault. I should have told you I didn't know how to dance. Please forgive me."

Phyllis giggled. "Don, one of these days when you and I are old and gray we'll look back on this occasion and have ourselves a good laugh. However, right now I'd settle for a corner to hide in."

Meanwhile, some Good Samaritan glued Phyllis' heel back on to her shoe and once again Her Royal Highness Queen Phyllis and her handsome escort Don Frady mixed and mingled with their friends.

When Queen Phyllis got home, Mama and Aunt Laurie were waiting—eager for a firsthand account of the entire event.

Mom and Dad

If Only I'd Stayed Home

Every year Mama looked forward to springtime. She drank in the flowering fragrance of magnolias and splashy rose-tinted crepe myrtles that intermingled with majestic oaks and yellow poplar trees. She delighted in looking out on the hillside and mountainside blanketed with flowering dogwoods and mountain laurel.

For Phyllis, her junior year in high school (1964) would forever be remembered with deep sorrow. Phyllis had barely turned 17 when Mama died. For a long time afterward, Phyllis blamed herself for going to school the day Mama died.

That fateful morning Mama was gasping for breath. "Mama," said Phyllis, "I'm not going to school today. I'm staying home to take care of you."

Mama managed a faint smile in between her gasps for air. "Phyllis, I want you to go to school. I'll be alright. I've had asthma since I was a child. This shortness of breath will get better as the day progresses."

Even though Phyllis had never known of her Mama's having asthma, she wanted to believe her. So, Phyllis went to school that day, but all morning long she had an unexplainable feeling that something awful was about to happen. It felt as if any minute a heavy iron ball was going to drop onto her head.

Around 10 o'clock that day the principal called over the intercom for Phyllis to come to the office. Phyllis rushed to the principal's office and soon was face to face with a family friend, Carolyn. Taking one look at Carolyn's grief-stricken face and not waiting for an answer, Phyllis blurted, "What's happened? Is Mama in the hospital? How's Daddy? Has someone died?"

Her friend gulped. "Phyllis, it's your mama."

Phyllis burst into tears. "Mama? What's wrong with Mama?"

Carolyn bit her lower lip. "Phyllis, your mama died this morning. I've come to take you to your aunt's house."

"NO! NO!" cried Phyllis. "It can't be. Not Mama. All day I've had a dreadful feeling that something terrible was about to happen." She paused. "I should have stayed home with her. This is all my fault."

"No, Phyllis, don't blame yourself. It isn't your fault. Your mama's blood clot happened so quickly, it wouldn't have mattered if she had been in the hospital or if there had been a phone nearby."

"I still wish I'd stayed home. Carolyn, where's Daddy? How's he holding up?"

"Your mama's death has hit him very hard. He thought, like all of us, that after her operation for her gall bladder she would gradually get stronger. Your daddy is making the final arrangements with the funeral home. He's coming back to your Aunt Laurie's house to meet you. I've come to take you there."

Phyllis clasped her hands together and closed her eyes. "Carolyn," she said, between sobs, "I want to go to see Daddy. He needs me and I need him."

When they arrived at Aunt Laurie's house, Phyllis thanked Carolyn and rushed inside. Daddy and Charles were sitting at a small table, talking with a group of men.

"Daddy!" called Phyllis. Both Daddy and Charles excused themselves and rushed to greet Phyllis. For the longest while the three of them remained in a prolonged embrace. In a cracking voice Daddy said, "Phyllis, you and Charles no longer have a home."

Phyllis began shaking her head, and her voice grew strong. "No, Daddy, that isn't true. As long as we have each other, we'll always be a family." It seemed to Phyllis that in just a few hours Daddy had aged 10 years. She feared they might lose him, too. "Daddy," she asked, "have you taken your heart medicine?"

"Not yet," said Daddy. "Right now, we need to finish making the arrangements for Mama's funeral. You can give me a shot after the funeral plans are completed."

The next day, as they were getting ready to leave for the viewing, Charles and Phyllis and their daddy shared their thoughts leading up to Mama's death.

Phyllis clenched her fists. "When the doctor made his rounds on the afternoon after Mama's surgery, he didn't bother to examine her or to ask if everything was okay. Before anyone could say a word, he was gone!"

Charles added, "On the day Mama left the hospital she complained to the nurse about having sharp pains in her legs."

All this time Daddy sat hunched over and lost in deep thought. Finally, he said, "Mama was always worried about money. When the doctor suggested she stay longer in the hospital she refused to do so." He sighed deeply. "It seems how much money we have and getting medical help are always locked in a struggle." Daddy hesitated before saying, "Gather up your things. We need to get to Cleveland."

A funeral service was held the following day at Cookson Baptist Church, with an internment afterward in the family burial plot. Long after their relatives and friends had left, the Edwards family remained. Phyllis whispered to Daddy, "We need to get home before dark." He reached for her hand, and the three of them slowly left the gravesite.

Upon arriving home, Phyllis and Charles began sharing their thoughts about Mama. Phyllis said, "When I'd be up late in the evening studying, Mama would show up with a glass of milk and some homemade cookies. 'I thought you could use some brain food,' she'd say."

Charles wiped away the tears spilling down his cheeks. "When they told me Mama had died, it blew my mind. All I could think of was hopping in my car and going to get her. Daddy snatched my keys and shook me, saying, 'It's true. Mama is dead.'"

Charles' voice became subdued. "It didn't matter how ornery I'd been, Mama always loved me. Mama's laugh was contagious. I'd say something silly just to get her started. Once Mama began laughing, it was hard for her to stop."

For the longest while there was a prolonged silence. Gone was the laughter.

That night Phyllis could not sleep. She could picture Mama being with Jesus and her being on the outside, wanting to join them. She prayed, *Lord, I want to love you like Mama did. I do, so much, want to see her again!*

For a period of time it seemed that the Edwards family just went through the motions of performing routine tasks without thinking. Phyllis, Daddy, and Charles exerted a tremendous effort just to stay alive.

Charles, who had moved in with his Aunt Laurie in Ocoee so he could be closer to his job in Cleveland, moved back home. He kept his job in Cleveland but also helped Daddy with farm chores. Daddy, a bachelor until he married Mama, knew the basics of cooking. Every morning the three of them would build a fire in the cook stove and Daddy would make biscuits while Phyllis dished up the eggs, bacon, and sausage. After breakfast Phyllis left for school and Charles departed for his job in Cleveland. For the major part of the day Daddy was left to clean up the kitchen, attend to outside farm projects, and take care of the laundry. Phyllis managed to get all her assignments completed before she left school each day so she could help out with the chores at home.

Daddy was always waiting when Phyllis got home and he'd ask, "How was school today?" He tried hard to be cheerful, but his stooped shoulders and vacant stare were dead giveaways. His hands trembled. "This house is like a graveyard without Mama. Lord, how I miss Lela!" Daddy squared his shoulders and took a deep breath. "Phyllis Ann, after you get settled in, I'd like for you to milk the cow and gather up the eggs."

"Sure, Daddy. I'll take care of those chores, but before I do, I'm going to check out your vital signs and give you a diuretic shot."

The months pushed their way forward and suddenly Polk County, Tennessee, became a riot of colors. The woods surrounding the Edwards' farm erupted with the bright golden blossoms of American beech trees and the myriad tints of the area's sugar maples.

One Sunday afternoon as Phyllis prepared to leave for her senior piano recital, Daddy surprised her by saying, "Why don't I drive you to your recital?" He smiled that wry smile of his. "I need to check you out and see if I got my money's worth since our fourth-grade pig deal."

Phyllis gave a good performance of her classical recital piece. While a crowd of friends encircled her after the concert offering their accolades, Daddy remained in the background.

They were well on their way back to the farm when Phyllis asked, "Well, Daddy, did you get your money's worth?"

Daddy grinned. "As a matter of fact, I got my money's worth and then some. That was some show you put on!"

Phyllis worried about Daddy. Lately his ankles were twice their ordinary size, and it was getting much harder for him to breathe. It seemed to Phyllis that Daddy believed his days were numbered. She told Charles, "It's like knowing a hurricane is about to strike and you feel you can't do a thing to stop it."

One evening after supper Daddy began coughing. The more he tried to stop coughing, the worse it became. He motioned with his hands in between spasms saying, "Quick, get me to the hospital. I can barely breathe."

Doctor Smith met Phyllis and Charles in the waiting room of the hospital wing where their daddy had been admitted. His face grew somber. "It seems it was only yesterday that your mother died, and now I have the sad duty to tell you your daddy's heart is worn out and his lungs are rapidly filling up with fluid."

"Please, Doctor Smith," said Phyllis, "can't you do something to keep Daddy alive?"

The good doctor mumbled, "There's only so much a doctor can do. Your daddy's life is now in God's hands."

Phyllis and Charles remained by Daddy's bedside as the days came and went. Instead of improving, though, Daddy's problems grew worse.

Death left a calling card in the wee hours of one morning. As Phyllis and Charles catnapped by Daddy's bedside, Phyllis felt someone shaking her. "Phyllis, wake up. I need to tell you and Charles something."

Upon hearing his name, Charles' eyes popped open. "What is it, Doctor? It's Daddy, isn't it?"

"Yes," said Doctor Smith. "Your daddy has passed away."

Phyllis began wringing her hands just like Mama did when she was overwhelmed with grief. "Charles," she said, "what are we going to do? First, Mama dies and seven months later Daddy is dead."

Charles squared his jaw. "Phyllis, are you going to stay in school?"

Phyllis nodded her head. "Although my future looks darker than Doomsday, I'm not ready to cast aside my dream of going to college."

Charles frowned. "I thought you gave up on Santa Claus several years ago. It takes a heap of money to get a college education."

"I sure could use a miracle," said Phyllis. "I'm hoping my grades will earn me a scholarship. I hear there're some colleges where you can get what they call a work scholarship."

"Sis," said Charles, "do you believe in miracles?"

Phyllis began nibbling on her fingernails. "It's strange you asked me that question. As you know, Mama believed that when she died she'd go to heaven and live forever with Jesus. For some reason, I'm finding it difficult to believe that. Charles, don't you ever think about death and the hereafter?"

"Yes, I do. But unlike you, I accept it without a stack of questions. I think your science book learning is interfering with your Bible beliefs."

Phyllis waited a long time before she answered. "Actually, what I've learned in my science classes strengthens my belief in life after death. I feel close to God when I think of how all the parts of our body work together. What I struggle with is how hard it is for poor people to pay for hospital care and prescriptions. Doesn't God care for poor people?"

Charles grinned. "Keep thinking, Phyllis. It wouldn't surprise me if you don't someday discover you and Jesus share the same thoughts."[3]

58

In the Spotlight

In 1964, football mania dominated the corridors of Polk County High School. Phyllis' classmates stopped by her locker in between classes to offer their congratulations for being nominated as the football queen. Sandwiched in between her well-wishers was her best friend Bennie.

"Congratulations, friend! You have the entire school buzzing. My entire family is coming Friday night, just to see you."

Phyllis blushed. "It's an honor to be chosen by the football squad as their queen. Tell your family I'll be by to see them after the half-time festivities are over."

The days flew by and early one Friday evening Phyllis watched as a bustling crowd of students, former students, teachers, family, and friends arrived early to lay claim to the best bleacher seats, tugging with them stadium seats and extra blankets. It soon became a loud partisan crowd.

At 7:30 sharp the band major lifted his baton and his fellow band members joined in performing a rousing rendition of the school fight song. As the band members marched to the sidelines, the players of both teams, with great pomp, made their entries and with the blow of the referee's whistle the fray began.

Not even a crushing defeat of Polk County High's Wildcats could dampen the spirits of the homecoming crowd. Phyllis—decked out in a long, flowing, white dress with a crimson red sash draped from her shoulder to her waist—slowly came forward on the arm of her escort, the football captain. Her attendants on the arm of their escorts arrived behind her. The principal placed a tiara on Phyllis and crowned her homecoming queen for 1964. Her escort gave her a kiss and pointed his finger toward a red-faced Bill Miller, Phyllis' current beau.

Later, when she joined Bennie's family in the bleachers, tears trickled down Phyllis' cheeks. "I only wish Mama and Daddy could have been here."

Bennie squeezed her hands and mumbled, "I thought the same thing."

Phyllis continued, "They probably couldn't have attended the game, but you can rest assured that once I got home Mama and Aunt Laurie would have demanded a play-by-play account of the whole affair."

After the football festivities were over for the year, Phyllis settled down to finishing her senior year with a flourish.

The principal of her school inquired of her, "Phyllis, what are your plans after high school?"

Phyllis dropped her head and in a half-whisper said, "I want to go to college. I've always dreamed of becoming a doctor."

A wave of shock registered on the principal's face. He cupped his right hand under his chin. "Honey, that's a long, hard row to hoe. I hope you have some other plans in mind, just in case becoming a doctor doesn't work out."

After the death of both of Phyllis' parents, the faculty of Polk County High School rallied around their star pupil to see that she had guidance toward attending college. Mr. Bingham, Phyllis' high school science teacher, planned a special trip for her to visit Vanderbilt University. "Mr. Bingham," said Phyllis, "this looks more like a city than a school. How many students does Vanderbilt have?"

Mr. Bingham chuckled. "A lot more than what we have at Polk High School. Several thousand students attend Vanderbilt, and their faculty is one of the best in the South." He paused before adding, "We're going to the science building for a seminar on the heart."

Once they were inside the science building, they were directed to take the elevator to the fourth floor. Phyllis was awe-stricken by the demonstration of seeing a beating heart in a jar and by listening to the speaker in the huge lecture hall. Cold shivers ran up and down her spine. *Wow! This is breathtaking. I'd love to spend the rest of my life in the field of medicine.*[4]

I'm a Senior!

Principal Rogers knocked on the door of Phyllis' biology class. "Excuse me," he said, "I need to speak with Phyllis Edwards."

When her teacher nodded his consent, Phyllis gathered her books and exited with the principal. Upon reaching Mr. Rogers' office, Superintendent Charles Lynn Bates extended his hand and said, "Phyllis, let me congratulate you on your scholastic achievements during your 12 years as a student in our Polk County schools."

Blushing, Phyllis dropped her head and managed to eke out a "thank you." Mr. Bates continued, "Mr. Rogers tells me you want to enter the field of medicine after you graduate. Is that correct?"

Phyllis again ducked her head but managed to mumble, "I'd like to, but I don't have any money to pay for a college education."

Mr. Bates squeezed her hand. "That's why I'm here. Tennessee Tech in Cookeville has a work-study program. Would you allow me to pursue getting you a scholarship to Tennessee Tech?"

Phyllis flashed a big smile, and her voice became animated. "Mr. Bates, please talk with Tennessee Tech in my behalf. This Polk County farm girl isn't afraid of hard work." She laughed. "The first job my brother Charles and I had was selling the eggs we gathered on our farm. Daddy let us keep our tiny profits."

The two gentlemen smiled and Mr. Bates promised, "I'll speak right away with the president of Tennessee Tech. Expect to hear from me soon."

Phyllis returned to class, more determined than ever to finish her senior year with a stellar performance.

The weeks and months passed swiftly. For Phyllis and the Polk County High School graduation class of 1965, their long-sought 12-year journey had ended. The graduation exercises began.

Principal Rogers announced, "Welcome, parents, relatives, and friends of the class of 1965."

As soon as he bestowed the honors due to class valedictorian Mickey Waters, he called for Phyllis Edwards, the class salutatorian, to join him at the podium. Phyllis, in her black-and-white graduation robe and flashing her now-famous dimpled smile, made her way to the podium.

Principal Rogers handed Phyllis a certificate while saying, "Phyllis, it gives me great pleasure to turn over to you this certificate of acceptance from Tennessee Tech and with it our sincere wishes that you will achieve all of your academic and future job goals."

Clutching her certificate close to her heart, Phyllis responded, "I'd like to thank all my teachers for helping me reach this point in my life. For each of you I'm most grateful." She smiled, ducked her head just a tad, and returned to her seat.

After the graduation service was over, Phyllis lingered long enough to receive the well wishes of her teachers and fellow students.

Pam reminded her, "Don't forget you and I are going to be roommates in September."

Phyllis left her schoolmates and friends and rushed to share her good news with her Aunt Laurie. In a short time Phyllis began packing her earthly goods into a dilapidated suitcase belonging to her mother.

College

1965-1969

A Summer of Transitions

The following morning Phyllis was up at sunrise and standing in the lane by her overstuffed suitcase when Uncle Harle arrived. Hopping out of his truck he said, "Miss Phyllis Ann, I see you're ready to stake your fortunes at Tennessee Tech. Climb inside my truck and I'll take care of your suitcase. We should get to Cookeville in three hours, more or less."

As they drove from Ocoee to Cookeville, Phyllis and Uncle Harle chatted about long-ago days when Phyllis was a child and her mama and daddy were still alive.

Uncle Harle, who loved to tease Phyllis inquired, "Are you going to share with your college friends your real name?"

Phyllis giggled. "Do you mean Phyllisie Ann?"

Uncle Harle began chanting, "Here comes Phyllisie Ann, with a whistle and a grin, groundhog grease all over her chin. Do you remember the time your daddy killed a groundhog and when your mama refused to cook it, he proceeded to do the job?"

Phyllis grabbed her nose. "Whew! I'll never forget Daddy and his groundhog. After taking one bite, even Daddy spit it out, declaring, "Lela, get rid of this varmint!"

The time passed quickly, and soon Phyllis and Uncle Harle were driving onto the entryway at Tennessee Tech. Uncle Harle's face grew somber. He slowed down and slipped a $20 bill into Phyllis' hand, saying, "I wish I could give you more." His voice cracked. "I hope you know how much it means to all your kinfolk that you're going to college."

Phyllis squeezed Uncle Harle's hands. "Thanks for the money. I love each of my kinfolk. When you get home, keep your ears open for any job openings. I'll need to work during our break for Christmas and during the summer."[5]

Uncle Harle parked his truck, and he and Phyllis made their way to the admissions office where a friendly, middle-aged lady met them. "Hello, what can I do for you?" she asked.

Phyllis introduced herself and her Uncle Harle and handed her admissions certificate over to the lady.

The registrar said, "Hello, Phyllis. I'm Rita Davis. I've had several letters about you from Superintendent Bates. Please have a seat. I have a few forms for you to sign." Turning to Uncle Harle, she added, "I'll call for a campus boy to help you get Phyllis' suitcase to her dormitory room."

Soon a young man with an impish grin appeared and helped Uncle Harle locate Phyllis' dorm and to deposit her suitcase in her assigned room.

Then Uncle Harle and the campus boy, Greg, returned to the registrar's office where Phyllis was completing her admission papers. Greg glanced at his watch. "It's chow time. Why don't I escort the two of you to the dining hall for a bite to eat?"

Uncle Harle rubbed his tummy. "That sounds like a winner to me. How about it, Phyllis Ann? Are you hungry?"

Phyllis blushed and whispered, "I'd like that."

Upon entering the dining hall all eyes, especially those belonging to the guys, were cast on the beautiful blond-haired, blue-eyed co-ed with a dimpled smile. Soon a group descended on Phyllis and Uncle Harle, pumping them with questions.

Greg stepped into the fray and announced, "There will be plenty of time later for you to get acquainted with Phyllis Ann Edwards from Ocoee. Right now, before her Uncle Harle leaves to return home, they'd like to have some lunch."

After he finished eating, Uncle Harle, with a glint in his eyes, said, "Phyllis Ann, it looks like you're among friends. I'd best be on my way home."

"Tell Aunt Laurie I'll start to work tomorrow in the biology lab as an assistant." Phyllis nuzzled up to Uncle Harle for one final hug.

After Uncle Harle left for Ocoee, Phyllis, hoping to push aside a sudden attack of homesick blues, meandered her way back to her dorm only to find she had company. Finding the door ajar and hearing music in the background, she flung open the door and yelled, "Audrey, get over here and give me a welcoming Tennessee Tech hug."

"We're going to have a great time together," said Audrey. "Who would have ever thought that two of the poorest kids at Polk County High are enrolled in college?"

Audrey ran her hands through her hair. "I'm going to make a prediction," she said. "Phyllis, with your dimpled smile and natural good looks, you're going to soon have fellows hanging around you like a swarm of bees making honey."

Phyllis shook her head. "You seem to have forgotten about my steady boyfriend, Bill Miller. I don't know how he does it, but he's rather effective at keeping other guys at bay when it comes to dating me."

"Speaking about Bill reminds me that once our summer session is over, several of our Polk County High School fellows will be on campus. Why don't you and I plan a welcome party for them?"

Phyllis' eyes sparkled. "That's a grand idea! She began counting on her fingers. There's you, Bill, Tommy, and me. Do you know of anyone else?"

Audrey answered, "I think there's seven or eight of us in all. I'll entertain the group with some piano music and if we're lucky, the guys will take us for ride and maybe buy us a Coke."

"Audrey," said Phyllis, "I'm envious of how well you play the piano. I've taken music for many years, but I can't play anything without having the sheet music. But when someone hums a line or two of a well-known song, you begin playing the complete song. I love the way you jazz up songs by adding extra notes."

"Phyllis," said Audrey, looking serious, "can you keep a secret?"

Phyllis grinned. "You'll never know if you don't try me. So quick! Tell me your secret."

"It's Tommy Daughtery," said Audrey. "He doesn't know it yet, but some day he's going to be my husband. Phyllis, do you and Bill have secret plans?"

Phyllis answered quickly. "Oh, no! Bill and I just hug and kiss a lot but we never, never talk about our future plans."

Friday meshed into Saturday, and Saturday into Sunday. On Monday morning Phyllis knocked on the office door of Fred Fox, professor of biology. A middle-aged man of medium height and sporting an unruly mop of red hair opened the door to his study.

"Hello, you must be Phyllis Miller. Mrs. Davis called me earlier this morning to tell me you arrived on Friday." Giving Phyllis a vigorous handshake, Professor Fox offered, "Please have a seat and we'll go over the details of your job assignment. Will this be your first job?"

Phyllis took a deep breath. "Professor Fox, I grew up on a family farm in Polk County. Even at a very young age I had jobs I was expected to do."

Professor Fox nodded his head. "I had in mind jobs you might have been paid to perform."

Phyllis waited a few minutes. "When I was in the fourth grade, I had my heart set on getting a piano. Daddy bought a piglet and told me if I'd take care of the pig every day that when the piglet became a hog, he'd give me the money the hog brought at the farmer's market for my piano."

Professor Fox smiled. "Did you fulfill your end of the bargain?"

Phyllis' head bobbled up and down. "I fed that pig slop every day for nigh on a year, and Daddy also kept his promise." Phyllis smiled. "You might say I earned my piano the hard way."

Professor Fox chuckled. "I'm beginning to understand why you've come to us with such high recommendations."

Phyllis continued, "During my junior year I worked as a clerk at Lay's Five and Dime Store in Cleveland. In my senior year I worked as a waitress in Ocoee. I've saved all the money I earned on both jobs."

"Phyllis, let's go to the biology lab and I'll go over with you what you'll be doing at Tennessee Tech."

Professor Fox held up a dirty petri dish. "Your job will be to make sure these containers used by our students and staff are very clean. The task consists of four steps: pre-soak, wash, rinse, and air-dry."

Phyllis touched the soft gooey agar attached to the petri dish. "Is it difficult to melt the agar?"

"Not if you pre-soak the dish in very hot water for at least 30 minutes. After you have cleaned the petri dish, rinse it in cool water." Professor Fox placed his hand on a table consisting of a row of racks. "The final step is to put the rinsed petri dish on the drying rack. Phyllis, your work this summer will be rather light, but when school opens in the fall you'll have lots of dirty petri dishes."

"Who will be checking to make sure I'm doing my job correctly?" asked Phyllis.

"Until you get the hang of it," said Professor Fox, "I'll be your inspector-in-chief. How do you feel about that?"

Phyllis smiled. "I like that! When classes resume next term, I plan to take one of your courses."[6]

The summer months passed swiftly. Before Phyllis knew what was happening, Pam arrived with two trunks and an assortment of odds and ends. That same day Bill Miller also arrived on campus. Little did Phyllis suspect how their arrivals would adversely affect her ability to concentrate on her studies.

Troubles Begin Multiplying

"Oh, Phyllis," exclaimed Pam. "Isn't this exciting? Just think: we're going to be roommates all year. I can hardly wait to line up a date with one of the upperclassmen." Pam swayed her body to and fro. "Phyllis, get ready to party, party, party!"

Phyllis frowned. "Pam, I think you're forgetting one major thing. We're here to get an education."

Pam raised both her hands. "I was afraid you'd say something like that. Phyllis, go ahead with your book learning, but I plan to major on having fun!"

No sooner had Pam unpacked until Bill Miller left a message with Phyllis' dorm mother. "I'll pick you up at five for dinner at the Rebel. The two of us have a lot of catching up to do—Bill."

Bill arrived at five o'clock and kissed Phyllis' outstretched hands. "Beautiful, what do you say we find ourselves a quiet parking spot after dinner?" He winked. "I'm hungry for more than food tonight. How about you?"

Phyllis blushed. "Bill, I'm hungry for more than food also. I bet together we can create a few sparks."

For the next few months Phyllis felt like she was traveling on a fast-speed roller coaster. She knew she needed to slow down and pay more attention to her studies, but between Pam's constant chattering sessions and Bill's weekend demands, Phyllis' study time became less and less.

Phyllis was worried. The formulas and equations for chemistry might as well have been written in hieroglyphics. While many of her friends sailed through college chemistry 101, Phyllis was not one of them. Clutching her midterm chemistry grade of D close to her breast, Phyllis rushed to her dorm and flung herself across her bed, burying her head in her pillow.

What on earth made me think I could someday become a doctor? Here I am flunking out of basic chemistry! Doctors have to take lots of chemistry courses. I might as well drop out of school and go back home.

Hearing the door open, Phyllis hopped up to wash her face. *I don't want Pam to know about my bad grade. She'd never understand.*

Pam, as usual, was bubbling over with party plans. "Phyllis," she exclaimed, "my friend Bruce has a friend he wants you to meet. What do you say we join them for a ride around town?" Pam squeezed Phyllis' hands, totally oblivious to her swollen eyes. "Don't you just love being in college?"

Phyllis frowned. "Pam, don't you ever think of anything besides dating and having fun?"

Pam's eyes grew large. She wasn't accustomed to this kind of talk coming from Phyllis. Her voice became testy. "Well, pardon me! I was just trying to put a little sparkle in your dull life. All you ever do is go to classes and work in that old lab." She crunched her shoulders. "Maybe the two of us aren't cut out to be roommates. What do you think, Phyllis?"

Phyllis bit her lower lip. "Pam, you'll always be my friend. However, I think you're right. We don't make good roommates. I'm currently at a breaking point with my chemistry class. If I don't get a better understanding of chemistry soon, I might as well call it quits!"

Pam grew somber. "Quitting because something is hard doesn't sound like you, Phyllis. I'll explain our problem to the person in charge of assigning rooms, and we'll switch roommates real soon." Pam shot Phyllis a mischievous grin. "There must be at least one other girl on campus who enjoys cracking the books." Pam reached over and hugged Phyllis, saying, "I'm not about to stand in the way of Polk County's first female doctor."

It wasn't long before Pam moved out and Carol Powell, a pre-med technology student, moved in. Carol and Phyllis made an excellent duo. Phyllis opened up to Carol about her problem with understanding chemistry. "Carol, I need to buckle down and not turn loose of my chemistry book until it begins to make sense. So, if you come in and I don't speak, please be understanding."

"Take as long as you need, Phyllis. I admire your tenacity."

For the next week Phyllis lived with her chemistry book in the library and in her dorm room. One evening she broke her self-incurred silence by exclaiming, "Eureka! Now I get it!" She shook Carol, who was in the process of falling asleep. "Carol! Carol! Wake up. I've finally figured out the ins and outs of chemistry." Rubbing her sleep-crusted eyes, Carol said, "Hooray for you! Now can I go back to sleep?"

A final semester test brought amazing results for Phyllis Edwards. Professor Skinner flashed a test paper in the air, saying, "Only one person in our class made 100. I'm pleased to say the person with a perfect score is none other than Phyllis Edwards!"

"Yes!" said Phyllis, pumping her fist into the air. *It's time for me to change my major from medical technology to pre-med.*

Thanksgiving had come and gone and Phyllis had a job at Miller Brothers, a department chain store, to coincide with her Christmas break. One day a high school student, even younger than Phyllis, bought an expensive necklace and brought it to Phyllis who was working at the hosiery counter. She handed Phyllis a plastic card. Puzzled, Phyllis glanced at the card with its long list of numbers and said, "Excuse me. I'll be back in a second."

Phyllis showed the card to her supervisor and asked what she should do. The supervisor laughed. "Oh, that's a credit card, and your customer is Agnes McGill. Her father is one of the richest men in Cleveland." Then the supervisor proceeded to show Phyllis the process for recording such a purchase. After the transaction had been completed and the customer had left, Phyllis said to her supervisor, "As my mama would say, 'What are they going to think of next? Who would have ever thought people would be buying things using a tiny plastic card?'"

Long before her temp job at Miller Brothers ended, Phyllis and her steady beau Bill began making plans as to how they would spend Christmas Eve through New Year's Day.

Bill told her, "Since you get off at three o'clock on Christmas Eve, we'll leave from Miller's for Ocoee. My family is looking forward to having you with us for our Christmas Eve celebration."

Phyllis blushed. "I'm planning to wear the beautiful scarf your grandfather gave me last Christmas." She dropped her head. "Maybe someday I'll be able to give gifts to those I love."

On Christmas Eve morning before she left for work, Phyllis stashed away enough clothes to last her for the upcoming Christmas holidays. At three o'clock she left Miller's and joined Bill, who was waiting for her at the exit door. Immediately they made their way to the highway leading to Ocoee.

They arrived at Bill's white-framed house on Stump Street shortly before supper. His mother and father gave the two of them a lively welcome. "Phyllis," said Bill's mother, "We're so happy you have chosen to spend Christmas Eve with us. Let me take your jacket while you have a seat by the roaring fire."

Phyllis glanced around the room, drinking in the beautiful Christmas decorations. "Mrs. Bates, I love your decorations. This scene by the fire would make a lovely Christmas card. I can't wait to see your Christmas tree!"

Bill, who until now had said little, rubbed his stomach. "First we eat and then we gather round the Christmas tree to exchange gifts."

"Bill is right. Dinner is piping hot and ready to be devoured. As soon as Bill's grandparents arrive, we'll eat."

It wasn't long before all their guests had arrived and the group gathered around the dinner table for a scrumptuous meal. Phyllis found herself awed as she compared Christmas at the Bates' house with the Christmases of her childhood. She fingered the real silverware and white napkins by her plate.

Bill's family is rich compared to mine. Then she smiled. *Oh, how I wish I could turn back the clock and for one more time hear my mama laugh! I wonder what she'd think of all this finery.*

Finally, Mr. Bates announced, "It's time to gather round the Christmas tree and share our gifts."

Mrs. Bates read the first name tag. "This package is for Phyllis."

Phyllis blushed. "I'm embarrassed. I couldn't afford to buy any gifts."

Mr. Bates, Bill's grandfather said, "Phyllis, I love that scarf you're wearing. Consider your gift as a love gift for keeping our Bill satisfied." He winked, adding, "Besides, we're all looking forward to the time you're no longer a guest but a member of our clan."

Bill urged, "Phyllis, open your gift so the rest of us can see what we're getting."

Phyllis squealed with delight as she unfolded a pair of designer jeans. She clutched them close to her breast. "I've never had a pair of designer jeans. Thank you, thank you!"

Mrs. Bates smiled. "While I'm at it, there's one other package here with your name on it. After you open it you might want to excuse yourself and see if they fit."

Phyllis wasted no time opening her new package that revealed a beautiful checkered blouse. She held it up for everyone to see. "Excuse me," she announced, "while I try on my new outfit."

Shortly, Phyllis rejoined the party all decked out in her designer jeans and new blouse. "Well," she exclaimed as she turned around slowly, "what do you think?"

"Phyllis, you look stunning and they're a perfect fit," said Grandmother Bates.

Bill whistled. "Merry Christmas to the girl who has stolen my heart."

After everyone had received and opened their gifts, Phyllis whispered to Bill, "We need to leave for Aunt Laurie's. She and Charles are expecting me to spend Christmas Day with them."

After a round of hugs and thanks, Bill and Phyllis left the Bates for Aunt Laurie's. However, Bill had other plans. He veered the car toward Ocoee's special lovers parking spot. "What do you say we catch up on a little smooching before I turn you over to your Aunt Laurie?"

Phyllis giggled. "That sounds like a super idea."

However, someone else was in the process of laying claim to the smooching spot. The claimants honked and honked on their horn until Bill, disgusted, reneged and turned around.

As they sped away, Phyllis recognized the occupants of the intruding car. Phyllis laughed. "Bill, that's Bennie and her boyfriend. We ought to go back and demand equal time."

Bill shrugged his shoulders. "Let them be. I'll find us a cozy spot close to Aunt Laurie's."

Soon Bill knocked on the door at Aunt Laurie's house. When Aunt Laurie opened the door Bill said, "I've brought your favorite niece to spend Christmas with you and Charles." He pinched Phyllis' nose and said, "I'll see you the day after Christmas. Maybe Bennie will be through smooching by then."

Once Bill had left, Phyllis' mind and heart began racing back to yesteryears. Tonight was like olden times—well, almost. She hugged Charles and Aunt Laurie, but the magic makers—Mama and Daddy—were missing. While her Aunt Laurie had upgraded her new dwelling with electricity, it paled in comparison to the Bates' property on Stump Street.

Charles commented, "I must say my little sister is turning into a lovely young lady. Are you still dating that puny specimen of manhood?"

Phyllis chuckled. "Are you referring to Bill Miller?"

"Yeah," said Charles. "He's the guy who is always hoping to become a star football player."

"That's true," said Phyllis. "However, he'll someday be an electrical engineer and make a very good salary. Besides, with Bill hovering over me, I don't have to worry about having a date for the weekend."

Charles grinned, "Good old reliable Bill. Sounds like he makes you feel safe and wanted. But is that love?"

Aunt Laurie interrupted. "We need to get some sleep. Charles, you're sleeping in my guest bedroom. And Phyllis, you'll be sharing a bed with me."

While no one was looking, Phyllis snuck back into the living room and placed her gift of Evening in Paris perfume for Aunt Laurie and a container of Old Spice for Charles under the Christmas tree.

Early on Christmas morning Charles and Phyllis joined Aunt Laurie in the kitchen where she was busy replicating a menu from Christmases past. "I'll make the biscuits," said Phyllis. "How about letting me fry the bacon and country ham?" offered Charles.

After eating a hearty breakfast, they gathered around Aunt Laurie's sparsely decorated tree and exchanged gifts. Aunt Laurie gave Charles and Phyllis each a tin of sugar cookies, saying, "I followed your mama's recipe, including a dash of love and laughter."

"I'm going to save mine until I get back to Tennessee Tech," said Phyllis. "That way I can savor my Christmas memories."

Charles grabbed his jacket and summoned, "Ladies, put on your heavy coats. I'm driving us to make some pop calls on our relatives."

"That's a good idea, Charles," said Aunt Laurie. "How does fried chicken and banana pudding sound for a late supper?"

Both Phyllis and Charles responded at the same time: "Yum, yum!"

After they had made their rounds visiting relatives, the three of them returned home. Once the meal was ready and everyone had cleaned their plates, Aunt Laurie seriously warned: "If you children fight over the pulley bone one more time, I'm going to spank both of you!"

Charles and Phyllis glanced at each other and burst out laughing. "Aunt Laurie, do you remember our Sunday fights over the pulley bone?" asked Phyllis.

"Oh, yes," said Aunt Laurie. "Who could ever forget those confrontations?"

The day after Christmas, Charles had to leave early to return to work. Phyllis remained with Aunt Laurie, visiting Bennie's family and dating Bill every night.

Like all good things, Christmas of 1965 passed quickly. Soon Bill and Phyllis were on their way back to Tennessee Tech. Since the college operated on semesters, both of them still had to take their midterm tests.

Phyllis was on her way out of the library when one of her classmates met her with a startling question. "Phyllis, why didn't you show up to take your exam?"

A terrifying look washed over Phyllis' face. She dropped her books to the floor, trying to absorb what she had just heard. She stood for the longest time, frozen with both hands covering her mouth.

"How stupid of me! Do you reckon Professor Skinner will believe me if I tell him I thought our test was at 3 o'clock instead of at 2:00?"

Her friend gave her a half smile. "What do you have to lose? If Professor Skinner doesn't believe you, you'll at least know you tried to make things right. On the other hand, if he accepts your explanation, you'll know firsthand what it means to be given a second chance."

"Clear my path," said Phyllis as she retrieved her books. "I'm on my way to see Professor Skinner."

Huffing and puffing, Phyllis barged into Professor Skinner's room where she found him sitting at his desk at the bottom of the long lecture hall, going over the test results tallied by his assistant student grader.

Phyllis, frigid with fear, made her way down 20 stairsteps to where he sat. She cleared her throat to get his attention. Professor Skinner frowned. "Hello, Phyllis. May I ask where you were two hours ago?"

Phyllis, with her knees knocking, took a deep breath and said, "A few minutes ago as I was leaving the library, I met my good friend and she asked me the same question."

Professor Skinner raised his eyebrows. "Well? What did you tell her?"

Phyllis didn't blink. "I told her the truth. I told her I'd been in the library studying since mid-morning and never once did it cross my mind that I was missing taking a test! Professor Skinner, could you be so kind as to let me take the test right now?"

Professor Skinner doubled over laughing. "Your story is too crazy not to be true! Yes, have a seat. You can take the test now."[7]

I Can Do It!

Like a row of falling dominoes, the ensuing weeks and months of Phyllis' freshmen year at Tennessee Tech fell into place. As the school year began ebbing away, Phyllis made several vital decisions. Convinced that chemistry was no longer a threat, she changed her major from medical technology to pre-med, bought a car, and secured a summer job.

She approached her college supervisor, Doctor Ashburn, saying, "I've given it a lot of thought and I'd like to change my major to pre-med."

With a twinkle in his eye, Professor Ashburn commented, "I'm sure you're aware pre-med is a more rigorous course of study and that the state of Tennessee doesn't have many female doctors."

Phyllis smiled. "Can I tell you a little secret?"

"I love secrets," said her advisor. "Keep talking."

"Since I was a child, I've wanted to be a doctor. I see changing my major to pre-med as a down payment on fulfilling my childhood dream."

Doctor Ashburn nodded his agreement. "I'll honor your request." He offered Phyllis his hand. "I can see it now. Someday a shingle bearing the name Dr. Phyllis Edwards will be proudly displayed and clients will eagerly seek your help."

Having secured summer employment some nine miles from Ocoee, Phyllis realized her current rattletrap car was already gasping for life. She eagerly sought the help of her brother.

Charles reminded Phyllis of her latest car incident. "I truly believe the good Lord sent one of his angels to watch over you when your brakes gave way."

Phyllis nodded. "You're right. I phoned the gas station from Aunt Laurie's house." Recalling that hair-raising time, Phyllis doubled over laughing. "There I was on a paved road five miles from the nearest gas station, trying to control my vehicle with the gears. Lucky for me, I didn't meet any other cars on the road."

"Not to mention that the gas station attendants, who were waiting for you, physically got in front of the car and stopped it!" added Charles. "For someone with so much school learning, you sure can get yourself into a mess."

"Speaking of messes," said Phyllis, "how about that Sunday morning when you showed off your new motorcycle?"

"As I remember it, you were still in your pajamas," said Charles, grinning.

Phyllis once again doubled over laughing. "You've got that right. We were having a whale of a time on our joy ride until we met the members of Cookson Creek Baptist Church. They were headed toward the church as we sped by them in the opposite direction, thoroughly enjoying our joy ride."

"Okay," said Charles. "We've both had our share of goof-ups. What's on your mind today?"

"I have $500 in my savings account and need your advice on buying a used car. Will you help me?"

"Yes, I'm happy to help. Let's begin by visiting the used car lots."

The first dealership they visited showed Phyllis a sleek-looking car that caught her eye. "How about this one, Charles?"

"Wait just a minute," cautioned Charles. "You never buy a used car without first examining its inner workings." He proceeded to lift the hood. Soon his face turned red. "It's just as I suspected. This car's motor is on the soon-to-die list!"

After a week of visiting car dealers, Charles and Phyllis settled on a late 1950s Ford. Charles shrugged his shoulders. "Like most used cars, you need to know a trick or two in case it gives you a problem."

Phyllis frowned. "Charles, let's get something straight. I'm not Daddy. What are you talking about?"

Charles laughed and opened the hood. With a wrench he began banging on the carburetor. "Always keep a wrench in the trunk of your car. If your car ever stalls, give the carburetor a wake-up call with the wrench. I promise you it will work every time."

Phyllis' "new" vehicle provided transportation to her summer job at the Delta plant in Conasauga, some nine miles away. Several Ocoee residents who also worked at Delta asked Phyllis if they could commute with her, which she agreed to.

At Delta, Phyllis' sole job was to inspect the seams of each jacket. If Phyllis found flaws in the seams, the jacket was returned to the proper person and the worker had to re-do the job.

One day Phyllis overheard some women talking during their lunch break. "I'm never going to reach my quota of jackets as long as that Edwards kid is around," said one of the ladies, her voice cracking with desperation.

Another lady's face turned red. She pursed her lips. "It galls me having someone young enough to be my child telling me what I'm doing wrong. I was sewing while she was still in diapers!"

However, Phyllis' commuter friends found her to be friendly and reliable. One day they were running late and the highway was crowded with commuters. They had just turned off the main thoroughfare when suddenly Phyllis' car sputtered and came to a dead halt.

"Oh, no!" said one of the ladies, "we're going to be late for work. Are you out of gas?"

"No," said Phyllis, "my tank is full. Excuse me a minute; I think I know how to get us going again."

The ladies punched each other in their ribs when Phyllis hopped out of the car and opened the hood and began banging with a wrench on the carburetor.

"I've seen it all now," exclaimed one of her riders. "She thinks she can give the motor a whack and everything will be okay."

After a short pause the motor began humming again. One of the ladies said, "Well, bust my britches. It worked! Phyllis, where did you pick up that little trick?"

"From my brother who learned it from our daddy." She paused. "You might say such knowledge runs in my family. Sit back, ladies. We'll make it to work on time, provided a cop doesn't catch us for speeding."

The sweltering heat waves, common to Tennessee's summers, accelerated in the close quarters of Delta Manufacturing. Phyllis found performing the same monotonous task day after day to be most boring. She confided to Bill, "The only good thing about my job is my paycheck."

One day the factory owner, who lived in New York, showed up at the Delta plant. His presence sent everyone into a tailspin. One lady lowered her voice and told Phyllis, "Something has gone wrong here at Delta. The top boss only comes when there is a big problem brewing."

The dizzy blonde, who was also the plant secretary and who was carrying on a romantic affair with the boss, made it her business to corner Phyllis every time the boss visited her workstation. She demanded that Phyllis give her a play-by-play account of every word he'd said. Phyllis resented her extensive questioning. She confided in one of the workers, "Why is she so interested in what the boss says to me?"

"Ever since he took her out on a date, she's had her heart set on winning his affections," said the lady. "Since you're young, pretty and single, I imagine she considers you a personal threat."

"Goodness gracious," said Phyllis. "She doesn't have to worry about me. The boss is old enough to be my daddy."

After he'd been there more than a week, the boss made one final stop by Phyllis' workstation. "Miss Phyllis," he said, "I have good news for you. You've been exonerated."

Phyllis, believing this to be a compliment, thanked him and went on with her work. But when she got home, she headed for the dictionary and looked up the word exonerate. Her jaw fell as she read, *exonerate: to absolve someone from blame for a fault or wrongdoing.* Her hands trembled. *All week long it never once entered my mind that my work was part of his investigation.* Phyllis giggled. *It's good to know that wherever the problem lies I'm exonerated!*

Hovering over East Tennessee, the heat rays of July showed no mercy. Sweat poured profusely down Phyllis' hair, cascading to her cheek as she crawled into the driver's seat and awaited the arrival of the ladies who were commuting with her.

"The good Lord have mercy!" said one of the ladies as she swiped her sweaty brow. "If it gets any hotter, I'll melt away."

"Honey," said another commuter, "rev your car and get us moving. Even moving hot air is better than nothing."

Brother-Sister Bonding

Phyllis' tenure at the Delta plant was over in August, and she immediately began focusing her mind on her sophomore year at Tennessee Tech. At school she delved into her studies while stoking her dream of becoming a medical doctor.

Meanwhile, Bill Miller, assured of his position as her one and only love interest, took control of Phyllis' extracurricular hours—and Phyllis gave him no resistance.

She continued settling in to college life and her academics, with a growing self-confidence in achieving her professional goal.

Her sophomore year was winding down when Phyllis talked over her summer plans with her brother Charles. "I hear Delta manufacturing company has moved to Cleveland," she said. "I'm going to apply for a production job that pays a minimum wage of $1.25 an hour."

"That's a good move," said Charles. "The faster you do your work, the more money you'll make. As Mama used to say, 'Glory be! Child, you'll be raking in the dough.'"

Phyllis applied for and got the job at Delta as a production assistant. Her job was to mark with chalk where the ladies were to sew on belt loops to army garments.

It seems Phyllis was always looking for a good used car. Alas! Knocking on the carburetor of her old Ford with her wrench no longer worked, so she set out on her own to buy another used car. Unfortunately, her new used car came with a set of tires just waiting to expire. One day when Phyllis was on her way to Aunt Laurie's house, one of the tires was obviously low. Exasperated, Phyllis called Charles and he left his job to come to her rescue.

Charles' face was grim as he examined all the tires on her car. "It looks like it's only a matter of time before all of your tires expire." He scratched his head, saying, "It's a good thing we have a gas station less than a block away." He hopped into her car and said, "I guess now is a good time to teach you how to add air to your tires. Drive us to the gas station and look for the sign that reads 'Free Air.'"

In a few minutes Phyllis parked her car by the Free Air sign. "What do we do now?" she asked.

Charles grinned. "So far, so good. Now watch carefully what I do." He then proceeded to follow his actions with step-by-step verbal directions. Turning to

Phyllis, he directed: "Now it's your turn. I want you to add air to your tire while I look on."

Phyllis took a deep breath and removed the screw-on cap from the tire. First, she used her gauge to see how much pressure was in the tire. Knowing the tire needed to be at 32 pounds, she attached the air pump into the opened slot. Beads of sweat popped up on her brow as she repeatedly sent gushes of air from the air pump until the tire gauge read 32. Glancing toward Charles she asked, "How am I doing?"

Charles smiled. "You're a quick learner. When both of us have a little extra time, I need to teach you how to change a tire. If you ever have to drop out of college, maybe we can get you a job as a mechanic."

Phyllis Pleads Her Case

During Phyllis' third year at Tennessee Tech, she was busy coordinating her final courses under the watchful eye of Doctor Ashburn, her pre-med advisor. As the year progressed, Phyllis participated in refresher course seminars, took the MCAT entrance exam required for admission to the University of Tennessee medical school, and paid her registration fee of $50.

Phyllis waited a second before saying, "Doctor, I have one thing left to do, and that is to fly to Memphis for a scheduled face-to-face meeting."

"I'm working on arranging that and will soon be able to tell you the time they have allotted for you," said Doctor Ashburn. "How do you feel about flying to Memphis?"

"I have mixed emotions," said Phyllis. "I'm very apprehensive over having the interview, and this will be my first trip on an airplane." She squeezed her hands and whispered, "I'll most likely be nervous."

As soon as an appointment date arrived for Phyllis to meet with the director of admissions at the University of Tennessee medical school, she proceeded to make her air travel plans. She arranged with her dad's cousin Lois to spend the night with her in Nashville and to fly a commuter plane to and from Memphis for her interview.

As Phyllis boarded the small plane in Nashville, she scrambled to find her appointed seat. As the engine began revving up, she clenched her fists. *Look at me. I'm as nervous as a cat on a hot tin roof. Let's hope the next 30 minutes pass quickly with no mishaps.*

Unfortunately for Phyllis, weather conditions didn't cooperate. Every time the plane hit an air pocket the tiny plane seemed to do flip-flops. *Good Lord of mercy! I wish I were back in Nashville.*

Gradually the turbulence ceased, and soon the plane landed. Phyllis pushed her way to be among the first to exit. She hailed a taxi to the medical school and after several inquiries arrived for her appointed interview with the director of admissions. True to her long-standing introverted silence, Phyllis greeted him with a smile but waited for him to pursue the interview.

"Welcome, Phyllis," the director said. "I hope you had a pleasant plane trip." He waited a few minutes before continuing. "Can you tell me why you want to go to medical school?"

Phyllis relaxed. "I've always been drawn to the medical field and am attracted to anything that deals with taking care of sick people." She paused before adding, "I appreciate the science of medicine that is involved in trying to figure out what is going on in a person's body. It intrigues me."

Soon the interview was over. The director thanked her, and Phyllis quietly made her exit. She called the Memphis airport and luckily was able to book a return commuter flight to Nashville that same afternoon. This time there was zero air turbulence. Within the hour Phyllis was back visiting with Lois.

"How was your trip, and how did your interview go?" asked her cousin.

Phyllis leaned back in her chair. "My ride from Nashville to Memphis kept me wondering if I would survive the ordeal." She ran her fingers through her hair before continuing. "I think I gave a good accounting to the director of why I want to become a doctor. He listened thoughtfully and thanked me for coming." Rolling her eyes, she added, "Whatever happens after today is out of my hands. The committee has possession of my scholastic work at Tennessee Tech and my MCAT scores. After today's interview I can't do anything more. From here on out it's a 'wait and see' time."

Lois handed Phyllis a cola. "While you quench your thirst, I'll begin putting the finishing touches on our supper. How does fried chicken, corn on the cob, green beans, and home-grown tomatoes sound to you?"

"Yum, yum," said Phyllis, patting her stomach. "Sounds like a love feast to me. How can I help?"

Upon her return to Tennessee Tech early the next morning, Phyllis was met by a small group of her closest friends, eager for her to bring them up to date. Phyllis, however, was cautious with her comments, not wanting to appear overconfident. Before the day closed, she had secured her nine months position as a ward clerk at Bradley Memorial Hospital in Cleveland along with keeping ajar the possibility she might be returning in the fall for a fourth year at Tennessee Tech. To Bill she confided, "Right now I'm keeping all my options open. Should the University of Tennessee medical school accept me, I'll have fun closing the doors I've kept open."

Bill nodded his agreement. "I've always known you were one smart girl." He reached over and gave her a quick kiss and affirmed, "Your job at Bradley Memorial sounds interesting."

The Letter

Phyllis moved in with her Aunt Laurie and commuted to her new job at Bradley Memorial Hospital in Cleveland on a daily basis. The first thing she did as soon as she got home every day was to check the mail. Phyllis was beginning to believe her application to medical school had been rejected, but then a letter appeared that sent her hopes soaring.

All her eyes could see were the words marked in red on the envelope: LETTER OF ACCEPTANCE. With tears cascading down her cheeks, Phyllis made a beeline to the house. She grabbed Aunt Laurie and twirled her round and round. "Aunt Laurie, the letter came! I've been accepted! I'm going to Memphis!"

Aunt Laurie grabbed her pounding heart, "Oh, dear me, you'll be so far away from home." Then she brushed away her tears and handed Phyllis the phone. "Share the good news with your friends." As an afterthought, unheard of by Phyllis, Aunt Laurie added, "You can settle up with me when the phone bill arrives."

"Carol, this is Phyllis. Are you ready for some good news? My letter of acceptance arrived in today's mail." What followed was a series of squeals, laughter, and unintelligible gibberish known only among female friends. An hour later Phyllis was still on the telephone sharing her good news. Aunt Laurie decided to butt in. "Phyllis, can you stop for now? You need to eat your supper. After all, you still have to go to work tomorrow."

As soon as Phyllis scanned her morning schedule, she leaned back in her chair and smiled as she dialed Tennessee Tech.

"Hello, this is Phyllis Edwards. Please connect me with Doctor Ashburn's office."

"This is Doctor Ashburn. May I ask who is calling?"

"Doctor Ashburn, this is Phyllis Edwards. I have some wonderful news!"

"That's terrific. Let's hear it!"

"My acceptance letter from the University of Tennessee medical school came in yesterday's mail."

Doctor Ashburn chuckled. "I suppose that means you'll want me to cancel your plans for returning to our campus?"

Phyllis giggled. "Would you please take care of it, Doctor Ashburn?"

"Phyllis, I'm happy to cancel your Tennessee Tech plans. Don't forget that I'm counting on you to stay in touch with me after you get settled in at Memphis. Is it a deal?"

"Yes, sir. You'll hear from me. Thank you for all the help you've given me. I couldn't have made it this far without you."

Phyllis hung up the phone and straightened a few objects on her desk before calling Bill Miller. She scratched her head. *I wonder how my news is going to register with Bill. I'm sure he'll be happy, but Memphis is a long way from Cookeville and Bill has one more year at Tennessee Tech before getting his engineering degree.*

"Hello, Bill. How are you this morning?"

"Hi, Phyllis. Getting a phone call from you is always special. What's on your mind?"

"Bill, my letter of acceptance from the University of Tennessee medical school came yesterday. Isn't that wonderful?"

There was a pregnant pause. "Hello, Bill. Are you still there?"

"I'm still here, Phyllis. That's great news and I'm very happy for you, but it upsets me knowing you'll be so far away."

"My being in Memphis while you're still in Cookeville will be rough for both of us. But gee whiz, we're talking about something that is eight and a half months from now. Right now, I'm counting the hours until I see you on Friday."

During their Friday date Bill said, "Phyllis, we've been sweethearts since we were juniors at Polk County High School."

Phyllis leaned her head onto Bill's shoulder. "That's true and for more than five years neither of us has dated anyone else."

Bill snuggled close. "Although we've never discussed it, I've always thought that someday you and I would marry."

Phyllis started to say something, but Bill continued talking. "I wish I could put a ring on your finger that would tell the guys in Memphis, 'Hands off, this girl belongs to Bill Miller.'"

Phyllis blushed. "Bill, you know you don't have to worry about me dating someone else. You can count on me to wait for you."

Bill smiled. "That's what I hoped you'd say. I plan to soon put in a request to be hired by a reputable Memphis engineering firm. If things go the way I'm hoping, we should be making our wedding plans before you begin your second 18 months tenure at the University of Tennessee medical school."

I Love This Job!

Meanwhile, Phyllis settled into her work at Bradley Memorial Hospital where she gained a bucketful of golden memories. When several of the doctors discovered Phyllis had been approved as a pre-med student at the University of Tennessee Medical School, they invited her to sit in on some of their surgical proceedings.

Stopping by her desk one morning one of the doctors said, "A patient of ours has a broken finger that must be repaired under anesthesia. Would you like to observe as we take care of her injury?"

Phyllis did not attempt to hide her enthusiasm. "That's wonderful! When will you be operating?"

The doctor glanced at his watch. "It's now 11 o'clock. Meet me in the observation section of our surgery room at 2:00."

Phyllis set spellbound as two of the doctors worked at resetting the broken finger. Her heart beat rapidly. *I can't believe this is happening. God willing, it won't be long before I'll be operating on my own patients.*

On another occasion she was allowed to observe as the doctors performed a D&C, and then she looked on as they performed an exploratory laparotomy—a surgical incision into the abdominal cavity for diagnosis. After asking a fistful of questions Phyllis told the doctors, "I can never thank you enough for allowing me to watch as you operate on some of your patients. I'll always treasure these firsthand experiences you have given me."

A male nurse named Larry took a liking to Phyllis and sought ways to help her make extra school money. "Phyllis," he said, "how would like to make some money by becoming a private duty nurse?"

Phyllis shrugged her shoulders. "I'm afraid that's impossible. I've had no experience as a nurse."

Larry winked. "With the case I have in mind, you won't need any experience. All you'll have to do is sit. Phyllis, the job pays well."

Against her better judgment, Phyllis agreed to take the job—only to find she'd been grossly misled.

When she arrived for her first sitting stint, the patient's doctor was in the room with her. When Phyllis introduced herself the doctor said, "Your patient has to be turned every hour." After a brief pause the doctor added, "Do you have experience as a patient sitter?"

"No, I've never had a job where I sat with a patient all night," responded Phyllis as she stared at the comatose form lying in the hospital bed. She gulped for breath before saying, "Did you say I need to turn her every hour?"

"Yes. Be sure you record any unusual sounds she makes." With that bit of advice, the doctor left.

Phyllis couldn't take her eyes off her patient. Shaking her head, she thought, *This isn't going to be easy. She's three times my size and so heavily sedated she doesn't know if it's night or day.*

After the first hour passed, Phyllis proceeded to move her patient. She embraced her patient and began tugging her forward. Alas! Every effort Phyllis made ended in frustration. When Phyllis pulled her patient forward, her body flopped backwards. Now Phyllis was perspiring. The lady's limp body refused to respond: 45 minutes later Phyllis had managed to at least move the lady's torso a bit.

Just wait until I see my friend. If he calls this an easy way to make money, I wonder how he'd describe a difficult task? If I make it through this night, I won't ever try this again!

With the coming of morning the patient's doctor emerged, asking, "What is your patient's temperature?"

Phyllis spoke up. "I don't know her temperature, and I haven't been trained to take someone's blood pressure."

The two parted company, and Phyllis made a beeline to find Larry.

Medical School

1969-1972

What Am I Doing Here?

On a windy morning in March of 1969, Phyllis Edwards left her aunt's house in Ocoee, Tennessee, bound for Memphis, some 400 miles away. The dream that had permeated her life since early childhood was on the cusp of becoming a reality. Would she succeed in becoming a medical doctor, or would she buckle under at the gate of opportunity?

Phyllis reported to the Goodman House, an old building close to the campus. After residing solo in her small cubical for a few days Phyllis made a friendship gesture to Dana, another female medical student. It wasn't long until they were attending all the orientation lectures together, sharing family stories, and cramming for courses they shared.

A meeting shortly after Phyllis had arrived at the UT medical school sent out a call for any students interested in being on a suturing team to attend a meeting under the direction of some senior medical students. Phyllis and Dana attended the open forum.

One of the senior medical students was troubled by their presence. He cornered the two of them, saying, "I don't think you understand. The patients at John Gaston Hospital are males with no insurance, and their manners are extremely crude. You really must have a thick skin to serve on the suturing team."

Phyllis smiled. "I understand the risk. Sign me up!"

Her first suturing job sent her into shock. A black male who was intoxicated and sporting bleeding scalp lacerations approached her.

"Stop dawdling. Hurry! Sew me up!"

As Phyllis reached for the numbing medicine, her patient grabbed her arm and let go a stream of profanities. "Did you hear me? Skip all that pain killer stuff and sew me up!"

Phyllis grimaced as she began suturing the burly gentleman's wound he'd received in a beer fight. When Phyllis pricked her patient's skin with her needle, he'd scream bloody murder and fill the room with curse words unfit for man or beast.

The day was well spent when she dismissed her patient. Wiping away the sweat that had accumulated on her brow and under her armpits, Phyllis declared to the world, *The Lord have mercy! I surrender. Somebody else can replace me on the suturing team.*

By the end of her first semester, Phyllis had convinced herself she'd never become a doctor. Secretly she harbored foreboding thoughts. *What am I doing here? I feel like a fish trying to swim without water. I'm going to quit after this semester and go back to Tennessee Tech. I'll get a degree in chemistry or biology and teach school in Polk County.*

At first Phyllis kept her self-defeating messages to herself. However, one evening she lay bare her feelings to Dana.

Dana turned on Phyllis like an attacking bobcat. "How dare you think of quitting! Don't you realize all of us are consumed by fears, some real and some imagined? Let's face it: Becoming a medical doctor isn't for the fainthearted. Forgive me if I'm not jumping in the middle of your 'poor Phyllis party.'"

Phyllis sat for the longest while stunned and unable to offer a decent rebuttal. Sensing she'd deeply hurt her good friend, Phyllis said, "Dana, I'm sorry—really sorry! I got wrapped up in my own problems and failed to realize we're all in this fishbowl of existence together. Please forgive me."

Dana hugged Phyllis. "That's what best friends do. We forgive our friends when they aren't thinking straight. You're the last person I'd suspect of giving up your dream. Do you have any idea how much I look up to you?"

Phyllis lowered her tear-filled eyes. "Dana, if you're not quitting, then neither am I. You're right. Becoming a doctor is no place for the fainthearted!" The two left, arm in arm for their next class.

Medical School Jitters

Phyllis' initiation to gross anatomy was navigated by Professor Kirkland, a flaming red-headed female. Professor Kirkland spoke to the huge gathering of medical students: "This course is a little different from courses you've taken up until now. I imagine some of you have never been in close contact with a dead body. Remember, the cadaver you will soon begin examining once belonged to a living human being and should command your reverence and respect."

Phyllis eyed the long, blue bags lying on stainless steel tables, all in rows. She trembled, feeling both apprehensive and thrilled. Retiring to the locker room, she changed from her street clothes into lab clothes—a scrub dress, a type of apron, some gloves, and shoes.

The large class had been subdivided into groups of six students, with no more than one female in each group. When she returned from the locker room Phyllis found her assigned group members, anxious for the next directive from their professor.

"Your first job," said Professor Kirkland, "will be to slice open the skin on the chest. Listen carefully to my instructions." When she had finished with the instructions she added, "Now it's your turn. Good luck."

For a while there was complete silence as the groups hunched over their cadavers, nervously eager to try their luck. After a while Phyllis and her peers gained enough confidence to move about the room to see how the other groups were managing their cadavers. Phyllis whispered to one of her friends, "Wow! This is like making my dream of becoming a doctor tangible."

One evening Professor Kirkland invited her female medical students to her home for dinner.

Staring at the exquisite table with its wide array of silver, Phyllis nudged Dana. "Have you ever sat down to eat with such an elaborate collection of utensils? How on earth will we know which utensil to use?"

Dana gulped before saying, "Professor Kirkland, thank you for inviting us to your beautiful home. We've been so busy studying to become doctors that our table manners aren't up to snuff. Perhaps you can help us navigate through the meal."

Professor Kirkland smiled. "If you make the same choices I make, you'll have no problem." She paused before adding, "If you girls can dissect a cadaver, then I think you can pour a cup of tea. As for which piece of silver to use, wait until you see which utensil I pick up. If you make a mistake, that's okay too."[8]

There was no way of escaping it. If you were in Professor Kirkland's gross anatomy class, you reeked with the smell of formaldehyde. Phyllis and her friends were constantly working to camouflage the pungent, acrid smell that penetrated their skin, clothing, books, etc. Regardless of what they did, the horrid smell remained!

One Friday, Phyllis and Dana decided to take in a movie. They scrubbed their bodies and shampooed their hair vigorously to try to get rid of the formaldehyde smell. They even dabbed on some perfume behind their ears and on their wrists, hoping to lessen the smell that haunted them day and night.

After they got on the elevator someone already on the elevator began sniffing. Finally, the sniffer said to her friend, "There must be some M1's (first-semester med students) nearby. I'd know that smell anywhere!"

After the girl with the snide remark got off the elevator, Phyllis turned to Dana. "I guess our camouflage efforts boomeranged. It's going to take more than a few drops of perfume to disguise our fated formaldehyde odor."

Phyllis was almost through her first year as a medical student when her monetary funds hit rock bottom. Shivering from the frigid December weather and wrapped in her tattered winter coat, she hit the streets of Memphis seeking a part-time job.

Christmas carols and jingling cash registers pervaded downtown Memphis. However, time and again Phyllis' inquiries came up empty. Distressed, Phyllis thought, *I feel lower than a treed bobcat. Unless I get a job, I'll have to drop out of school.* That's when her thoughts turned to John Gaston Hospital.

She went straight to the desk of the clerk in charge of job placements. "Hello," she said, "my name is Phyllis Edwards and I'm a medical student looking for a part-time job. Do you have any openings?"

The clerk scanned her list of unfilled positions and then replied, "We have one position open." She scowled before adding, "It's the urine room. Are you interested?"

Phyllis didn't bat an eye. "Yes, I'll take it. Can I start today?"

"Yes, you can," said the clerk. After Phyllis had completed the necessary paperwork the clerk called to a young man, saying, "Please take Miss Edwards to the urine room."

Phyllis did a doubletake as she entered the smelly, small room surrounded by stack upon stack of pungent urine specimens and a few microscopes. In a few minutes a young student intern arrived and went over with Phyllis her duties before explaining, "If you do a good job in the urine lab, you might get to go out on the floors to draw blood and afterward run tests on one of the lab machines."

Phyllis thanked the intern. He left and she began her work. After spinning a specimen in a centrifuge, a rapidly rotating machine, she examined the sediment under a microscope and then followed through by sending a report to the patient's room.

Phyllis held her nose and mused, *If this is what it takes for me to stay in school, then I'll become the best urinalysis technician in town!*

Phyllis learned a lot about the human body from observing urine specimens at John Gaston. It wasn't long before she was trusted to go on the floor, draw blood, and then bring it back to the lab and run whatever test had been ordered.

For one semester Phyllis had to work three 12-hour shifts one week and four 12-hour shifts the next week. The long hours caused her grades to plummet. Finding out that several other pre-med students were having the same problem, she and her colleagues devised a plan where during the night one person would stay awake for a couple of hours while the others slept.

One night during Phyllis' time slot to work, she received a spinal fluid specimen to analyze. She examined it under the microscope, counted the number of white blood cells indicative of infection, did a simple math calculation, and issued her report.

Shortly an intern resident doctor knocked on the door of the lab and asked Phyllis, "Are you sure your count of white blood cells is accurate? My patient has meningitis. If your report is true, then it indicates he's much improved and I will stop his antibiotics." His face became drawn as he added, "If your white blood cell count is wrong, then my patient will die!"

With the intern hovering over her shoulder, Phyllis did the count again. The results were the same as she had reported. Saying nothing, he left. Phyllis was perplexed. She repeated the test numerous times and every time got the same results. *If I'm wrong, a patient might die!*

When it was time for Phyllis' shift to end, she asked her friend who was taking over to doublecheck her work. Much to her relief, he confirmed she was correct and also cautioned: "If I were you, I wouldn't worry about your resident intern critic. He's known for giving pre-med girls a hard time."

Medicine and Matrimony

Late in the evenings, after they had finishing studying, Dana and Phyllis often stayed up to the wee hours of the morning sharing stories. Frequently they talked about their sweethearts.

"It's so hard being here when our boyfriends are miles away."

"Dana," said Phyllis, "I have something I need to tell you."

"Yes. Let's hear it."

"Do you remember when I went through that terrible episode when I told you I was going to leave medical school and return to Tennessee Tech?"

"You bet your booty I do."

Phyllis lowered her voice. "It's true I found the sheer volume of our casework overwhelming. However, the main reason I wanted to leave was Bill Miller. I was so homesick for him I couldn't see straight."

"That doesn't surprise me. But aren't you glad you stuck it out?"

"I shudder when I think how close I came to leaving," said Phyllis. "Thank you, Dana, for showing me how mixed up my thinking had become."

The grind of Phyllis' first 18 months as a medical student was four months away when Bill, grinning from ear to ear, arrived one morning around 10 o'clock at Phyllis' apartment. He was clutching an envelope in his right fist. Bill swept Phyllis into his arms and after a prolonged kiss pulled away slightly. He thrust the envelope into her hands and announced: "Take a look at this. You're looking at the newest employee of Schering-Plough, one of the top firms in Memphis."

Phyllis squealed, "I'm so proud of you." She rolled her eyes and tickled his ribs. "I guess that means you can now take me out to a real restaurant."

"Honey, this contract means we can set our wedding date. Are you ready to become Mrs. Bill Miller?"

"I'm more than ready. How does June 20 sound to you? That would give me time to make my wedding dress and to plan the wedding."

Phyllis left Memphis by car a week before the wedding for Aunt Laurie's house in Ocoee. Spotting Phyllis' car from afar, Aunt Laurie was standing in the driveway when Phyllis arrived. After playing "catch up" with the news, Phyllis showed Aunt

Laurie her wedding gown, a white satin dress with long sleeves. The one item left to create was her veil. Phyllis parceled out that job to her future mother-in-law.

"Bill's mother has made arrangements with Pastor Arms to perform the wedding, and she asked several ladies and me to help with the wedding reception," said Aunt Laurie. "Have you and Bill invited those who will be in your wedding party?"

Phyllis retrieved a tattered list. "Please go over this with me. I'm thinking it's complete." Phyllis began reading from her list. "My friend Dana is my maid of honor, and Bennie is in charge of the bride's book. I've asked Patsy Poston to play the piano and Marilyn Hixson to sing 'Have I Told You Lately That I Love you?' The pianist will play Lohengrin's, 'Bridal Chorus' as Charles walks me down the aisle. And when the ceremony is over, she'll play Beethoven's 'Ode to Joy' as we exit. I've asked my cousin Roberta's daughter, Lucy, to be my flower girl."

"Little Lucy," said Aunt Laurie, "reminds me of you when you were five. She's awfully shy. Don't be surprised if she backs out at the last minute."

"I'll doublecheck with Lucy and her mom today." Phyllis giggled. "Aunt Laurie, it doesn't seem fair. All Bill has to do is to show up at Cookson Creek church with his best man, Tommy Daughtery, but I have a list of things to worry about."

Phyllis couldn't have been too uptight over the pending event. Two days before their wedding the bride-to-be and her future husband, oblivious to the world, were seen on a borrowed motorcycle racing madly up and down the lanes and roadways of Ocoee, Tennessee.

It was the day before the wedding. Phyllis had just finished eating breakfast and was helping Aunt Laurie in the kitchen when the phone rang.

"Hello," said Aunt Laurie. "May I ask who is calling?"

"Aunt Laurie, this is Roberta, Lucy's mama. May I speak with Phyllis?"

Aunt Laurie, with a worried look, handed the phone to Phyllis.

"Hello," said Phyllis. "How are you?"

"I'm fine but I'm having a terrible time with Lucy. She's bawling so loud she's driving me out of my mind. She says she's not going to be the flower girl at your wedding and that I can't make her." Roberta sounded desperate. "Phyllis, I feel lower than an inchworm over this. Do you mind asking cousin C.W.'s daughter Linda to be your flower girl? I hear Linda is a born performer."

Phyllis thanked Roberta and assured her, "I'll call C.W.'s wife Peggy right away. Believe me. I understand Lucy's fears."

"Hello, Peggy. This is Phyllis. I have a great big favor to ask of you and Linda."

"I hope we can help you, Phyllis. What's on your mind?"

"Roberta's daughter Lucy was going to be my flower girl in my wedding, but at the last minute she's refusing to perform. I'm wondering if Linda would be my flower girl?"

Peggy chuckled. "Linda loves to perform. Hold on and let me clear this with Linda." In a few seconds Peggy was back on the phone. "Linda is so happy that you asked her to be your flower girl, she's turning cartwheels in the living room!"

"Thank you so very much," said Phyllis. "The wedding is this coming Friday. We'll be having a rehearsal tomorrow afternoon. I'll see you and Linda tomorrow."

On the day of the wedding the church was packed with family and friends, and everything went as planned except for one minor exception. As Linda followed Phyllis down the aisle, her feet got tangled in the hem of her long dress and she fell to the floor. Unfazed by the mishap and holding her container of rose petals, Linda hopped up and resumed her trip to the altar rail.

After the wedding reception the newlyweds changed into more comfortable clothes and left for their honeymoon—a one-night stay in Atlanta, Georgia. They spent the rest of their honeymoon riding on Lake Ocoee in a boat belonging to Phyllis' brother Charles.

Upon their return to Memphis, Bill had to attend to mundane things such as learning the ins and outs of a new job while Phyllis had a tiny frame of time to adjust to her new role as a wife. Their newlywed life included some funny incidents.

Phyllis, wanting to make the first meal she ever cooked for her husband to be special, went shopping and found a white fish filet that was much cheaper than the other fish. She bought the fish and cooked it for their supper.

When Bill took a healthy bite of it, his face turned red and he shoved his plate aside. "Honey, I'm sorry. I can't eat this!"

The fish that was so cheap had been caught locally and wasn't edible. They scraped their plates and headed for the closest hamburger joint.

On another occasion Phyllis put a turkey in a plastic roasting bag. She must have "fowled up" the temperature gauge. She and Bill were in the living room when suddenly they heard a series of loud POWS and BANGS! Dashing to the kitchen,

Bill jerked open the oven door. Phyllis' turkey, unharmed, lay in a split-open roasting bag. It took both of them several hours to clean up the oven walls that had been splattered with grease.

On Thanksgiving Day the newlyweds were dining with Bill's parents in Ocoee. Phyllis asked her mother-in-law, "What can I do to help?"

"You can take the turkey out of the oven," replied Mrs. Bates.

Phyllis, intent on maintaining her approval rating with Mrs. Bates, opened the oven to retrieve the turkey in the big roaster. She accidently tilted the pan, and the turkey rolled out onto the floor!

Mrs. Bates put her arms around Phyllis and reassured her. "Don't fret. You're worth more to us than a hundred turkeys." Then Mrs. Bates bent down to survey the extent of the damage.

She leaped up and grabbed Phyllis' hands. "You aren't going to believe this! Mr. Tom Turkey landed safely; all we have to do is wipe up the juices that managed to escape."

Phyllis snatched a towel from the rack near the sink, dampened it, and went to work cleaning up the excess spillage.

"Phyllis," confided Mrs. Bates, "this incident will be our little secret. No one but you and I need ever know this happened. Help me move the turkey to the dining room table."

Phyllis sighed. "Thanks, Mrs. Bates. "This is the second fowl that has created chaos for me. If Bill ever gets wind of this, I'll never hear the last of it."

St. Jude Children's Research Hospital

St. Jude Children's Research Hospital, founded by actor Danny Thomas in 1962, is recognized throughout the world for its pediatric treatment and research facility that focuses on children's catastrophic diseases, particularly leukemia and other cancers. Treatment is free of charge to the patients.

In 1970, Phyllis had a three-month break between her first and second 18 months of medical school, so she jumped at the opportunity to involve herself firsthand with the young cancer patients at St. Jude's and to make herself available to the institution's massive research center.

Phyllis was impressed with the caliber of international doctors who chose to work there. She was assigned to Doctor Aur from Brazil.

Doctor Aur, his countenance glowing with confidence, extended his hand to Phyllis. "Welcome to St. Jude's. If you expect this to be a depressing place to work, you'll be wrong. Our children are brimming with hopeful smiles and are trusting us to change their dreadful chances."

"Thank you, Doctor Aur. I have a lot to learn, and I'm looking forward to having your esteemed help to guide me." She paused momentarily. "I'm ready whenever you are to begin seeing our patients."

Doctor Aur ushered Phyllis into a room where she was introduced to an eight-year-old youngster. As Phyllis turned to say something to the child's parents, words failed her. The child's parents, like rigid robots, were glaring daggers at each other.

When they were well outside the child's room, Doctor Aur said, "I saw you picking up on the tense frowns the boy's father and mother were exchanging." He shook his head. "While our patients pay nothing for their treatments, their parents often accumulate massive expenses due to the time they lose from their jobs." He paused before adding, "It's not uncommon for parents to blame each other for their child's condition." Then he held his hands to his lips and said softly, "The beautiful parents are those who throw cost to the wind and spend their time encouraging their youngster to get better."

One of the patients Phyllis encountered was 16-year-old Katy. She was sullen, angry, scared, uncooperative, and refused to open her mouth during visits. But on one of the visits Phyllis accidently found near Katy's bedside table a magazine devoted to horse trainers. "Katy," she asked, "do you like horses?"

Katy glared at Phyllis. Her words were harsh. "Before this (blankety-blank) cancer claimed my life I had hopes of becoming an equestrian." Suddenly her visage softened and tears began streaming down her face. "Will someone tell me when I'm going to die?"

Doctor Aur remained silent, allowing Phyllis the opportunity to intervene.

"Katy, I don't blame you for being angry," said Phyllis. "Life has dealt you a crushing blow. Won't you please give us a chance to help you?"

"But you don't understand," said Katy. "Cancer is cancer and I'm going to die!"

Doctor Aur interrupted, saying, "Katy, all cancers are not equal. Actually, you have a form of cancer that is treatable. With your help we don't have to totally squash your horse trainer's dreams."

Katy, her chin quivering said, "I guess I've been too ornery. Doctor Aur, what do you suggest?"

As the days and weeks passed, Phyllis detected a metamorphic change in Katy. She met their visits with smiles and had an open attitude toward Doctor Aur's treatment plans. Even though Katy's disease eventually took her life, she was able to come to grips with her disease and destiny. Katy elected to devote the remaining days of her life to sponsoring equestrian events for St. Jude's.

Tiny five-year-old Melissa, with her vanishing blond hair and fetching blue eyes, had been in and out of St. Jude's for more than a year. During her stays in the critical care unit she'd endeared herself to the staff. Phyllis was no exception. Knowing Melissa wouldn't be around in December, the staff planned a Christmas party for her in October.

On the day when Christmas came early, Melissa and her mom wore matching red velvet dresses trimmed in faux white fur. Melissa had a tiny sprig of mistletoe tucked in her headband. Her eyes seemed to dance with anticipation. She squeezed her tiny hands under her chin.

"I love Christmas! Will Santa pay us a visit?"

Doctor Aur, waiting in a nearby closet, recognized his cue. Phyllis smiled as he emerged with a string of gutsy "Ho-ho-hos." Phyllis, dressed as Santa's elf, began unloading Santa's pack. Soon Melissa was surrounded by a pile of gifts: a giant teddy bear, a cuddly doll, several puppets, a stack of story books, simple wooden puzzles, crayons, and coloring books. Meanwhile, the staff who showered the happy child and her mother with gifts and hugs were reluctant to have the party end.

In less than a month Melissa died.[9]

No Place for the Fainthearted

Phyllis' first 18 months of medical school had been consumed with studying anatomy, microbiology, and blood chemistry and lots of bookwork and labs. Her second 18 months consisted of clinical rotations through such disciplines as medicine, surgery, pediatrics, obstetrics-gynecology, and orthopedics.

Under the supervision of licensed doctors at John Gaston Hospital, Phyllis worked with indigent patients. The wards at John Gaston were large rooms consisting of many beds lined up against the walls, with only curtains dividing the patients.

One of the medical school's professors was fond of testing the skills and honesty of the students. An eye exam was capable of revealing a lot about the patient's health. In a normal situation when a medical student shined a penlight at the patient's pupil the eye would constrict. The professor often confronted his med students with a patient he had implanted a glass eye. Many of the med students gave the professor textbook answers, though there were exceptions.

"Phyllis," asked the professor, "what happened to the patient's eye when you shined the penlight on it?"

Timidly, Phyllis replied, "Nothing, sir. I've repeated the test four times and get no response."

The professor probed, "Are you sure you saw no pupil movement?"

Phyllis nodded her head and handed him the penlight. "Why don't you try?"

The professor smiled. "Congratulations! I'm proud of you. There's nothing wrong with your skills or your honesty."

Phyllis rubbed one of her hands across her chin. "I don't understand."

The professor chuckled as he gently removed the fake eye. "You didn't get a response because your patient has a glass eye."

When Phyllis arrived at work each day, she never knew what kind of crisis might be waiting to erupt. But squashed between the serious were sometimes humorous incidents.

Phyllis' team was assigned to an elderly lady with vaginal bleeding. Phyllis began probing in the lady's pelvic area until her agile fingers detected a foreign object. Slowly she brought the object out for examination.

It was hard for Phyllis to keep a straight face as she turned to her patient and handed her a tube of lipstick. "This is the source of your troubles. As long as you keep from shoving beauty products up your vagina, you shouldn't have any more bleeding problems."

The obese woman exclaimed, "Well, I never!" Cackling like a hen that had just laid an egg, she added, "Would somebody please tell me how that happened?"

Phyllis and her team members joined in the laughter. Phyllis shrugged her shoulders. "We were hoping you might tell us how a tube of lipstick wound up in your vagina."

The obese patient stopped laughing. Rolling her large brown eyes, she declared, "There isn't any telling. I reckon I must have been on one of my drunken sprees and thought it was a tampon. Thank you, honey child, for taking such good care of me. If you'll excuse me, I'll be on my way home."

A harder case involved a viral male patient who upon coming across an abandoned moonshine still proceeded to help himself. It wasn't long before he arrived at John Gaston with symptoms of diarrhea, nausea, and vomiting. It fell Phyllis' lot to exam him.

The disheveled patient looked as if he'd just left a violent tornado and barely survived the ordeal.

Phyllis thought, *How unlucky can I be? I get to examine a male patient with a group of male med students watching every move I make.* She shrugged her shoulders. *I'm going to be careful and never let any of them know how embarrassed I am.*

Turning to her patient she inquired, "What seems to be your problem?"

The patient released a string of curse words. "That's a crazy question."

Suddenly he began upchucking and expelling odious gases. "For your information, you might like to know I got drunk. Now, will you do your examining so I can get some relief?"

Phyllis winced and, while a covey of male medical students congregated behind her, she began to give the man a rectal exam. Throughout the examination the passage of liquid stool and horrendous stink bombs abounded.

Undaunted by his vitriolic insults and odious smells and ignoring the tittering that came from the galley, Phyllis told her patient, "The booze you drank was poisonous. We'll pump the contaminated liquor out of your system and give you a series of pills to take. A week from now you should be alright."

The old curmudgeon yanked up his pants and glared at Phyllis. "You doctors are all alike. You have a pill for every ache and pain." He snatched the prescription out of Phyllis' hands and gingerly returned to his bed.

As the final phase of Phyllis' second year of medical training drew near, she found herself delivering many babies and loving every minute of it. At first her baby deliveries were done with her supervisor directing her actions step by step. However, it wasn't long before her supervisors, realizing Phyllis was adept at birthing babies, remained close by just in case they were needed.[10]

When one of Phyllis' African-American patients was shown her new infant, the new mother wailed: "Doctor Miller, you're fooling me. There's no way this can be my baby. This baby has pink ears. My baby has brown ears."

"I can assure you," said Phyllis, "he's your baby. All newborn African-American babies have pink ears. Give him a few weeks and his ears will be as dark as a bar of chocolate."

The new mother slowly rolled her eyes and took her newborn in her arms and drew him close. Phyllis overheard her saying, "Honey child, don't you fret. I'll keep your ears covered until they turn as brown as a gingerbread cookie."

During their break time Phyllis turned to Dana and asked, "When are you and Gene getting married?"

"One month after graduation," she replied, her eyes sparkling. "We'll spend our honeymoon in New York City. While Gene finishes his doctorate in psychology, I'll be doing an internship in pediatrics at Mount Sinai hospital in Manhattan."

Phyllis gave Dana a quick hug. "I'm thrilled to hear about your future plans, and I'm sure you'll do well at Mount Sinai. It's been so good having you as a friend and roommate during med school."

Suddenly a lump formed in Phyllis' throat. Dana nudged Phyllis, saying, "Hey girl, you and I are friends forever. You do remember Ma Bell, don't you? All you'll have to do is to dial my number and say, 'Dana, this is Phyllis. I need to talk.'"

Capturing a Dream

One of the soon-to-be medical school graduates motioned for Phyllis to join his group. "Hi, Phyllis. Come join us. We need your help. We're having a discussion over reciting the Hippocratic oath as part of our graduation service."

"What's the problem?" asked Phyllis. "Are some of our students opposed to reciting it?"

Another fellow jumped into the conversation. "It's worse than that. For some reason our administration has deleted the oath from our graduation ceremonies, and we're trying to come up with an alternative plan. How do you feel about us gathering as soon as the service ends in the room just off the main entrance to recite the oath together?"

Phyllis smiled. "That sounds perfect. The Hippocratic Oath is symbolic of why I became a doctor! Count me in."

The cavernous auditorium buzzed with activity as parents and friends arrived to wish their sons and daughters well. Phyllis, decked out in her black graduation gown, anxiously kept her eyes peeled toward the front entrance.

"Look, Bill! There's Charles and Aunt Laurie." She rushed over and embraced them. "Look at you. You two are a sight for sore eyes! I'm so glad you came."

Soon Bill's parents arrived. Smiling Phyllis exclaimed, "The Edwards-Bates-Miller clan is present. Let the ceremonies begin!"

The music from the grand organ soon began swelling throughout the auditorium, and Phyllis hurriedly slipped into her assigned spot. Solemnly the 100 doctoral candidates began marching down the long hallway and took their assigned seats down front near the podium. After the rendition of special music came remarks by the dean of the medical school. Then the inspirational speaker issued a challenge to the new doctors. Last, but most important, came the granting of diplomas.

One by one the candidates marched across the stage to receive their diplomas. There was a brief pause between each presentation. With her face glowing and her blue eyes sparkling, Phyllis stepped forward as the director called, "Phyllis Miller, Ocoee, Tennessee."

Upon receiving her diploma, Phyllis returned to her assigned seat. As she waited for the remaining diplomas to be awarded, her thoughts turned to her childhood.

Mama, Daddy, I hope you hear me. With God as my witness, I promise you I'll work so that poor people get the same treatment as those with money!

At the conclusion of the commencement exercises Phyllis said to Bill, "Bring our family with you and meet me outside the room near the auditorium. I won't be long."

Phyllis quickly aligned herself with those students wanting to include the Hippocratic oath as part of their graduation experience. Someone called the group to order, and those assembled recited in unison and with conviction:

I solemnly pledge myself to consecrate my life to the service of human-ity. I will give to my teachers the respect and gratitude that is their due; I will practice my profession with conscience and dignity. The health of my patient will be first consideration. I will respect the secrets that are con-fided in me, even after the patient has died. I will maintain by all means in my power, the honor and noble traditions of the medical profession.

My colleagues will be my brothers. I will not permit considerations of religion, nationality, race, party politics, or social standing to intervene between my duty and my patient.

Professional
&
Personal Life
1972-1998

Rejection Ignites Acceptance

After marrying off her good friend Dana and sending her and her husband off to New York City, Phyllis turned her attention toward her first year as a rotating intern at Baptist Hospital in Memphis, Tennessee. In this setting she was designated to spend a couple of months in each of several disciplines: obstetrics-gynecology, internal medicine, surgery, and pediatrics.

Because of her growing skill and interest in the OB-GYN field, Phyllis found herself spending more and more of her time checking on the patients in the labor and delivery area. In cases involving surgery, she would evaluate the patients and then scrub in and assist with their surgeries. She became adept at performing surgeries and was convinced she'd found her niche in the medical profession. The OB part was appealing to Phyllis because it dealt with patients (babies) at the beginning of life.

The months sped by, and soon her first year at Baptist Hospital was about to end. It was time for her to declare her area of expertise. Phyllis talked it over with Bill and also called Dana.

"Hi, Dana," said Phyllis. "This is Phyllis and I need to talk."

"I'm all ears," replied Dana. "What's on your mind?"

"It's time for me to declare my area of specialization, and I've decided on OB-GYN."

Dana said, "That doesn't surprise me. Go for it!"

Phyllis hesitated. "There's just one potential drawback. The final decision as to whether I'll be accepted or rejected at Baptist Hospital lies in the hands of our infamous Doctor Shrier, the placement director for OB residents."

Dana retorted. "I'm glad I never met the old windbag with his indecent views on women."

"Dana, I need to come up with an alternative plan in case he turns me down. Do you have any suggestions?"

There was a pregnant pause before Dana responded. "Do you remember when that group of hospital specialists came to visit while we were still in medical school?"

Phyllis' eyes lit up. "Yes, I do remember! The man in charge at Erlanger in Chattanooga, Tennessee seemed to take a liking to me."

"Well, Phyllis, it seems you have your plan B. If Doctor Shrier turns you down, you should immediately contact Erlanger."

"Thanks, Dana. That's exactly what I'll do. Say hello to Gene for me."

Doctor Shrier was a fixture at Baptist Hospital. Now in his late 80s or early 90s, he daily was seen in the doctor's lounge pontificating his philosophy on life. Since he had self-appointed the majority of the hospital's OB-GYN intern doctors, no one dared to openly oppose his remarks, even if they didn't agree with him.

A self-proclaimed bachelor, Doctor Shrier felt men should not be limited to one woman but rather they should have one as a homemaker, another one for social occasions, and of course one or several for satisfying one's sexual urges.

The opinionated doctor waited until the lounge was teeming with interns before saying, "Hey, you guys, listen up. The best present you can give a woman on her 40th birthday is her uterus in a jar." He rolled his eyes and added, "Don't waste your time or hers. Give her a hysterectomy and you'll prevent a lot of future problems."

While women and sex were his favorite topics, Doctor Shrier also delighted in expounding his atheist views on religion. Some people might find his stance a little ironic since he served on the staff of a Baptist hospital.

Phyllis heard him say, "I'll believe in God when you prove to me that he died and came back to life." He grimaced. "As far as I'm concerned, resurrection talk is just a lot of wishful thinking. We'd be a lot better off if we built more hospitals and fewer churches."

Some of the newer doctoral residents grew weary of Doctor Shrier's non-stop diatribe on religion. It was difficult to decide whether he was speaking from a well of bedrock beliefs or from being fearful of his own final destination.

Despite the possible obstacles she might encounter with Doctor Shrier, Phyllis knew she must declare her intended field of expertise. So, she spent the better part of a Sunday afternoon in September of 1973 assimilating her impressive OB-GYN credentials. When she'd collated all of them, she shared them with Bill.

"Honey, what do you think? Will I get the job?"

"It all depends," said Bill, "whether Doctor Shrier wants the best available candidate or if he'd rather drop dead before hiring a female for the position."

Phyllis grimaced and her voice bristled. "I hope you haven't forgotten my Plan B. If Doctor Shrier turns me down, I'll reroute my OB-GYN credentials to Erlanger Hospital in Chattanooga."

The following morning Phyllis took a deep breath as she handed her résumé over to Doctor Shrier's secretary and then left to attend to some other matters. Two days elapsed and Phyllis had heard nothing. Finally, someone posted a small typed notice on the community bulletin board. It read: "Doctor _____ (a male) has been awarded the OB-GYN position."

Biting her lower lip to masquerade her bitter disappointment, Phyllis hastened home and initiated a phone call to the chief in charge of OB-GYN personnel at Erlanger.

Someone answered the phone quickly. "Hello. This is Doctor Binder speaking."

"Hello, Doctor Binder. My name is Phyllis Edwards Miller, and I graduated a year ago from the University of Tennessee's medical school. Since then I've spent one year of internship training here at Baptist Hospital. Would you be interested in seeing my résumé?"

"Phyllis, my answer is yes! I remember talking with you when we made our annual visit to your alma mater. Send me a copy of your résumé and I'll get back to you in a few days"

"I'll get it in the mail to you today," said Phyllis. "Thank you very much, Doctor Binder."

Two days passed and Phyllis was getting ready to leave home when the telephone rang. She picked up the receiver and meekly squeaked, "Hello. This is Phyllis."

"Hello, Phyllis. This is Doctor Binder from Erlanger. You'll be getting a written reply in the mail, but I thought you'd like to know that our Erlanger placement staff is very impressed by your résumé. We'd be happy to have you join us for a brief interview."

Phyllis' voice lightened, and it was hard for her to remain composed. "That sounds very good, Doctor Binder. How would an appointment with your staff this coming Friday at 2 o'clock work for you all?"

"That's perfect. Phyllis. Consider it done," replied Doctor Binder.

The staff session on Friday went extremely well, and soon Phyllis was the proud owner of a contract between herself and Erlanger Hospital.

The Reign of Doctor Howard

Phyllis' belongings were still in disarray in July of 1973 when she checked in with Doctor Binder at Erlanger Hospital in Chattanooga. After 10 minutes of exchanging personal pleasantries, he said, "Two years ago we added Dr. Peggy Howard to our staff to oversee our OB-GYN teaching program. Phyllis, you'll answer directly to Doctor Howard. I think you'll find her to be demanding but fair. Come with me and I'll introduce the two of you."

Phyllis took one look at Doctor Howard, and troubling thoughts began swirling through her mind. *I suspect the road ahead is going to be rocky. Doctor Howard looks like a drill sergeant, and I bet she hasn't smiled in a year.* With her head slightly downcast, Phyllis extended her hand to Doctor Howard.

Skipping the formalities, Doctor Howard—a no-nonsense "do as I tell you" kind of person—said, "Welcome to Erlanger's OB-GYN residents' teaching program. I'm totally committed to my work and expect the same from you. Second best will not be tolerated. Do you understand?"

Phyllis blushed. "Yes, ma'am. I understand."

Doctor Howard, with her closely cropped hair and standing straight as a ramrod, continued. "Very good, I'll see you Monday morning at 7 o'clock sharp. Remember, I run a tight ship and frown on late arrivals!"

With that warning issued, Doctor Howard lit a cigarette and returned to her office desk.

Phyllis made sure she had an ample amount of coins on hand before heading to a nearby phone booth and placing a call to her friend Dana in New York.

"Hello, Dana. How are things with you at Mount Sinai?"

"Hello, Phyllis. It's good to hear from you. My supervisor is very strict," said Dana, "but that's okay with me. She's determined that we learn the best possible skills attached to becoming a pediatric doctor. How's it going with you at Erlanger?"

"Dana, I'm worried. Doctor Howard, my program director, sends cold chills up and down my spine. I live in mortal fear that I might unintentionally do something that doesn't measure up to her standards."

"Phyllis, stop doubting your abilities. I predict you and Doctor Howard won't have any major disagreements. If I remember correctly, you are also highly focused on your work."

Phyllis, encouraged by Dana's remarks, said, "As usual, you're right. I guess when all is said and done, I can live with her barking out orders like a drill sergeant if her instructions make me a better doctor." She paused before adding, "It's good to talk with you, Dana. You're better than a nerve pill to help me settle down. Let's stay in touch."

For the next six months Phyllis and her residency group of nine—two women and seven men—united under the demanding, charismatic spell of Doctor Howard. No one, including the Erlanger staff, dared to ruffle her feathers. Doctor Howard was Doctor Howard—period!

She never overtly praised a resident doctor for a job well done. On the other hand, she was quick to censure shoddy work. Phyllis, while being spared from any overt personal criticism from Doctor Howard, like her fellow residential doctors, was subjected routinely to being corrected.

Phyllis had done minor surgery on a patient one morning and waited until the end of the day to check on her patient. She discovered her patient was bleeding internally. Phyllis called her senior resident doctor. "I need your help. My patient's life is in peril!" Fortunately, Phyllis and her senior resident peer were able to stop the excessive bleeding and the patient survived with no further complications.

The next morning Doctor Howard called the entire crew of resident doctors together. "We nearly lost a patient yesterday. God forbid that you become mere clock punchers. Always stay with your patients until you're positive they are going to be okay!" Having issued her ultimatum, with neither a word of censure nor praise for Phyllis, she lit up a cigarette and returned to her office.

Doctor Howard was rabid on the subject of finding doctors with exposed strands of hair lurking out from under their surgical caps in the operating room (OR). Armed with her trusted shears, she examined each of the resident doctors' bouffant surgical caps. Even a trace of hair outside one's surgical cap elicited a response! Confronted with exposed hair, Doctor Howard sought no one's permission. Snip, snip went her scissors and then she glared at the guilty party.

"Your hair, even if you just washed it, is loaded with bacteria. Even a wisp of hair can contaminate an operation!" She thrust a couple of dollars in the guilty party's hand. "Go get yourself a haircut."

Betsy was the only other female resident in Phyllis' class. Phyllis and Betsy's personalities, while not antagonistic, were definitely not compatible. Betsy was very idealistic and laid back and tended to see the world through rose-tinted glasses. Phyllis, on the other hand, was highly focused and a team player who respected those in authority. She was determined to excel.

Doctor interns were required to work in many clinics within Erlanger's fast-expanding facility. Betsy had no car and did not know how to drive. She was in danger of having the wrath of Doctor Howard swoop down on her.

One day Betsy cornered Phyllis with a bold request. "I've got a king-size problem. Will you help me?"

Phyllis blinked her eyes. "What's bothering you? Has Doctor Howard again snipped a wad of your hair in the operating room?"

"It's more serious than that," replied Betsy. "If she finds out I don't have a car and don't even know how to drive, there isn't any telling what she may do to me."

Phyllis said, "Let me get this straight. You want to buy a car and you want me to go with you to pick one out?"

Betsy began nodding her head. "Would you go with me, Phyllis? I know absolutely nothing about buying a car!"

Phyllis, recalling her trips while at Tennessee Tech when her brother helped her pick out a car, agreed to the request. "Consider it done. First we need to go over our work schedules and find a time when both of us are free."

As luck would have it, they discovered they were both free on the upcoming Saturday.

Soon, Phyllis and Betsy arrived at a dealership not too far from Erlanger.

"Good evening, ladies," said the car salesman. "How may I help you?"

"My friend is looking for a good used car," said Phyllis.

The middle-aged salesman, with his hair slicked back to a greasy shine and sporting a double-breasted suit, motioned: "Follow me. I have just the car you're looking for."

When they finally found a car within Betsy's price range, Phyllis whispered, "Betsy, ask to look under the hood."

Betsy, however, wanting to show her independence from Phyllis, said to the clerk, "Please open up the trunk. I need to check it out."

With a puzzled look on his face, the salesman opened the trunk for Betsy's inspection. Then he asked, "Would you like to test-drive the car?"

"Yes," responded Betsy. "I'd like to drive it around in the parking lot."

"Pardon me," said the salesman, "but did you say you want to drive it around in the parking lot?"

"That's what I said," said Betsy. "Do you have a problem with that?"

Glancing toward Phyllis and grinning, the salesman quipped, "Not at all." He handed Betsy the keys.

Betsy made one loop around the small parking lot and bought the car on the spot. When all the paperwork was completed Betsy turned to Phyllis and said, "Thank you, Phyllis for coming with me. Please say a little prayer that I'll get back to Erlanger without having a wreck or getting a traffic ticket."

Phyllis rolled her eyes. "Betsy, do you have a driver's license?"

"No, Phyllis. Why would I have a driver's license when I don't know beans about driving?"

Once the initial shock at what she'd heard wore off, Phyllis mumbled, "May the good Lord have mercy!"

Somehow Betsy managed to navigate her way back to Erlanger and subsequently to drive herself without any mishaps to her health care assignments. When Phyllis shared her car-buying episode with others in her group, they whooped and hollered. Alas! Someone had pulled one over on their powerful program director, Doctor Howard.

There is no such thing as normal in an emergency room. Literally anything can happen on any given day. Phyllis had been seeing patients in ER for many hours, including a rape victim. When her duty time elapsed, she returned to her call room and fell fast asleep. In the wee hours of the morning her phone rang.

"Phyllis," said the emergency room doctor, "I hate to do this but I need you to return to the emergency room. We have a patient who is saying she's been raped by Jesus Christ!"

Phyllis rubbed her sleep-encrusted eyes. "Did I hear you right? Did she tell you she was raped by Jesus Christ?"

Phyllis crawled out of bed, traipsed down to the ER room, and signed the necessary papers declaring that the mentally ill girl had not been raped. Without further comment, Phyllis returned to her sleeping quarters—hoping the girl received the mental help she needed.

Roe v. Wade, a highly controversial bit of legislation having to do with a woman's legal right to an abortion was enacted in 1973, six months before Phyllis arrived at Erlanger. Upping the anxiety level, the staff and resident doctors had conflicting opinions about abortion.

Erlanger, a public hospital, was obligated to take care of everyone. Some doctors pushed for abortion procedures to become part of the residents' training program while others felt it was against their religious principles to perform an abortion.

The staff and resident doctors worked hard when dealing with those wanting an abortion to fulfill the patient's wishes rather than their own. This was easier said than done, however.

One day Doctor Howard told a young lady, "The decision whether to abort or not is yours, and we'll comply with your wishes. However, I want you to know that you alone may be making this decision but there are at least two others whose wishes you should consider."

The young girl had a blank stare on her face as she asked, "Who besides myself needs to be considered?"

Doctor Howard replied, "The guy who got you pregnant and the unborn child."

Making the abortion clinic separate and optional for resident doctors solved the abortion law for Erlanger Hospital. Residents who wished to provide abortions for their patients, now a legal right upheld by the Uited States Supreme Court, were free do so. At the same time the wishes of residents who preferred not to perform abortions were also honored.

Doctor Howard, upon reaching retirement age, resigned from Erlanger in January of 1974, and Doctor Binder took over as the interim director of the residency program until Doctor Braun was hired.[11]

With his protruding belly, Doctor Braun often arrived to work clad in a ghoulish yellow-gold suit that prompted off-color remarks from many of the resident doctors and nurses. "How gross! Here comes Doctor Braun in his yucky yellow suit. Somebody needs to change his diaper."

Often Phyllis was drawn into situations involving calculated risks. Braun's warped opinion of himself as a ladies' man made many of the nurses uncomfortable. They urged Phyllis to register their complaint. However, Phyllis ignored their plea.

Referring to the most handsome male doctor at Erlanger, she teasingly asked, "Would you be making this complaint if our favorite Romeo doctor was showering you with attention?"

The specter of legalized abortion was fodder for extensive discussions at Erlanger and throughout Hamilton County. Being located in what is commonly called the Bible Belt, feelings often incurred the wrath of protesting anti-abortionists.

While Phyllis was technically, by choice, eliminated from performing abortions, she was amenable to becoming involved when the life of one of her patients was endangered. If she determined that the patient stood a good chance of dying if the baby wasn't delivered early, she talked it over with the woman.

"In order to save your life, we must deliver the baby. I can't tell you whether your baby will live or die. However, you can be sure I'll do everything I can to save your baby. Every minute we wait increases the risk factors for your survival. Can I begin?"

If the patient agreed, labor was induced. The premature baby may be still born, but the mother would live.

Phyllis always felt it was her obligation to make sure her patient understood all of the available abortion options at her disposal. One of her patients in her second trimester decided to terminate her pregnancy because her baby had a severe fetal anomaly.

Phyllis commiserated with the gut-wrenching decision her patient was facing. She told her patient, "While no one can speak with certainty about an unborn baby, the chances your baby will be severely mentally and physically impaired are extremely high."

"Doctor, what would you do?"

"Professionally, I'm not allowed to share my opinions with you. All I can do is to tell you there is a clinic in Atlanta that takes cases such as yours."

Her patient chose to go to the clinic in Atlanta and later shared her experience with Phyllis. "Those screaming people outside the clinic were pounding on the window of my car shouting, 'Baby killer! Baby killer!' Doctor Miller, it isn't fair. All my life I've wanted to have a baby."

Phyllis' face grew grim. "Those protesters anger me, too. They love to rant and rave as if all of our patients are jumping up and down with glee, anxious to kill an unborn child. It's been my experience that most of the people seeking abortions are broken-hearted over the convoluted choices they have to make."

Through the years Erlanger Hospital has produced many outstanding mentors. One of those in the 1970s was Doctor Binder, whom the residents held in high esteem. He had a somewhat grandfatherly image of himself in regard to the young doctors he supervised.

Phyllis jokingly confided to one of her fellow resident doctors, "I don't think Doctor Binder gives us much credit for street smarts. He worries about us when we're off duty as well as when we're doing our hospital duties."

"That's true," replied one of the guys. "I must confess I kind of like having somebody around who cares for me as a person."

Doctor Binder was the moving spirit behind many of Erlanger's advances as a medical facility in the 1970s. He coupled being a visionary with getting things done.

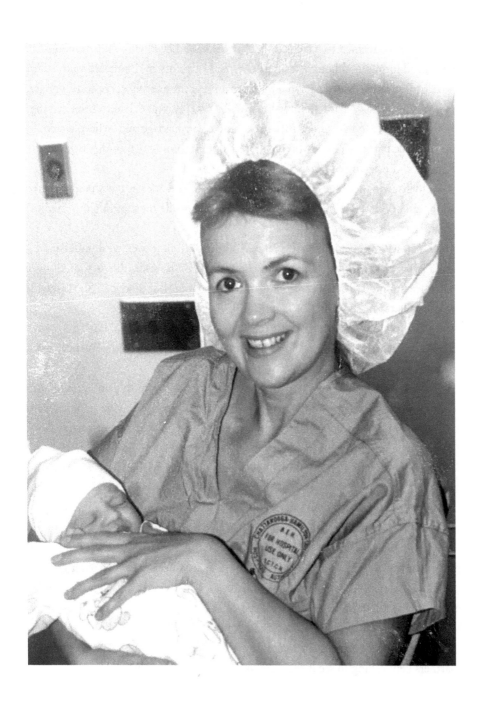

Climbing the Career Ladder

The shy little first grader who always ducked her head when she had to interact in new situations seemed to have vanished by the time Dr. Phyllis Miller emerged at Erlanger Hospital. Although women OB-GYN doctors in Tennessee were still a novelty, Phyllis cultivated a good reputation among the existing doctors at Erlanger.

In 1975 Dr. Millard Ramsey said to Phyllis, "Bob and I have been talking. Both of us feel we have more patients than we can manage and believe we could use a female partner. Would you be interested in becoming the third partner of the Ramsey and Boatwright practice?"

Phyllis, with her blue eyes dancing, responded, "Let me get this straight. You're asking me if I'd like to become a partner with one of the most prestigious medical teams in Chattanooga?"

Doctor Ramsey nodded. "If you need time to think it over, we'll understand."

Phyllis clasped her hands to her chest. "Doctor Ramsey, this is something I don't need to mull over. I'd consider it an honor to join your practice." She laughed, revealing her dimpled chin. "When do I move in?"

"We'll have a few adjustments to make," answered Millard, "but I'd say you should be an official member of the Boatwright, Ramsey, and Miller medical practice within three months."

Thus, Phyllis became a part of one of Chattanooga's most popular and successful medical practices. While working at Erlanger, most of Phyllis' patients were indigent. In private practice her clientele covered a broad spectrum of society from lower class and poorly educated all the way to the elite. Regardless of their socio-economic status, though, each of Phyllis' patients received the same high quality service.

Phyllis had not been with her new practice but a few days before she was presented with a tremendous challenge. It had fallen her duty to cover and care for the firm's patients who were in labor. She had to simultaneously attend not one but three women. It didn't make it any easier that each of her patients were either professionals or married to professionals within the Chattanooga area. This was quite a contrast to the indigent patients she served as a resident.

With the wealthy women, as she had done with the poor, Phyllis moved quickly from patient to patient as she waited for their labor to progress. Meanwhile, her partners kept calling to see if she were okay or if she needed help.

"Doctor Boatwright," said Phyllis, "tell Doctor Ramsey I have things under control." She took a deep breath and continued, "After this episode is over, I think I'll be fully initiated into the world of private practice!"

Early on, Phyllis was approached by one of the doctors about becoming president of the OB-GYN Society in Chattanooga.

Phyllis was astonished. "This is a joke, isn't it? Me, the president of our OB-GYN Society?"

"No, we're dead serious. All of us were impressed with the scholarly paper you recently presented to our group."

Phyllis raised her eyebrows. "Are you aware this would make me the first female to ever occupy the position?"

"Yes, we are," said Doctor Hutcheson, "and that is precisely why we need you. Your group of peers find you to be congenial, knowledgeable, and highly dedicated to your profession."

Phyllis accepted their offer and became the first female president of the OB-GYN Society.

Marriage and Motherhood

While Phyllis' career continued to climb, her urge to start her own family was like an incurable itch that couldn't be contained.

One day as she and Bill were walking to visit with some friends, Phyllis said, "Look, Bill. Aren't those kids adorable?"

"Phyllis," responded Bill, "what's so special about a group of kids playing kick-ball?"

Phyllis tugged on Bill's arm. "Honey, wouldn't it be wonderful if we had a baby?"

"Good grief, Phyllis. You must be out of your mind. With your schedule as it is, when would you have time to take care of a baby?"

Stunned by Bill's lack of enthusiasm, Phyllis continued. "Bill, for the life of me there are times when I don't understand you. I thought you'd be strongly in favor of us starting a family. I could get a leave of absence and we could hire someone to watch the baby when we have to be away."

Bill shrugged his shoulders. "When we have a baby, both of us can kiss our personal wants and whims goodbye. Babies take over a marriage and demand center stage."

"Bill," Phyllis said, "I'm 29! Let's face it. I don't have forever for you to become enthusiastic. I want a baby—my baby, your baby, our baby."

It wasn't long before a jubilant Phyllis took her own pregnancy test and announced to all her family and friends that she was pregnant. *Listen up, world. I'm going to have a baby, a drooling cooing baby, all my own.*

Alas! In less than 10 weeks Phyllis' hopes were crushed.

"I'm so very sorry," said her doctor. "You're going to lose your baby."

Phyllis' face grew grim. "No, doctor. There must be some mistake. My baby is alive! Do you hear me, Doctor? This can't be happening to me."

Dismayed, heartbroken and crushed, Phyllis shared her loss with a few of her girlfriends and colleagues. She also confided with her senior resident friend Dr. Jim Sherrill and his wife Lenda. Finally, she told Bill.

Unable to deal with the inevitable, Phyllis inwardly capitalized her grief while pretending to others she had everything under control. *Like Daddy used to do, I'll keep a stiff upper lip. I'll go about my work as usual and pretend this never happened. Work, work, work! They'll never know how deeply I'm hurting.*

When it was time for Phyllis to have a D&C, a friend who had lost a baby prematurely took her to the hospital and stayed with her. Where was Bill? He did as he did every day: He went to work, seemingly considering the whole affair a minor event.

Despite Bill's lack of emotional support, Phyllis still held fast to her romanticized, Pollyanna dream of marriage. *Once I have a baby, Bill will become a perfect father. Don't all marriages end happily ever after?*

Phyllis stalled getting pregnant again while taking her board exams and working long hours in her new position with Doctors Boatwright and Ramsey. Several years elapsed before she again became pregnant. Even after she was certain she was pregnant Phyllis kept quiet, fearful she might have another miscarriage. She had been pregnant for four months before she told anyone—even Bill.

At her announcement, Bill stared at her in total disbelief. "How long have you known you were pregnant?"

"Four months," announced Phyllis.

"Four months? You waited four months before telling me you were pregnant? Why did you wait so long?"

"Frankly, Bill, I wasn't sure how you'd take it. You are happy, aren't you?"

Bill gestured with his hands. "How I feel doesn't count for much these days."

For the next five months Phyllis was on cloud nine. She kept close tabs on her food intake and continued her normal work schedule. Her euphoria was catching. Even Bill, who seldom got excited, became more attentive.

Rachel Miller made her debut on March 27, 1979, and her mother became 32 the following day.

Phyllis exclaimed, "This is the best birthday present of my entire life. My baby, she cooed. Can I hold her?"

The nurse in charge placed the tiny bundle of life in Phyllis' arms. "Say hello to your little girl."

Instinctively, Phyllis counted her fingers and toes. Soon the nurse retrieved Rachel, saying, "She'll visit you again when you get assigned to a room."

Phyllis turned and grabbed Bill's hands. "Isn't our little girl beautiful?"

Bill hemmed and hawed and finally said, "Yes, she's beautiful."

It wasn't long after Phyllis and baby Rachel returned home that Phyllis began noticing Bill's absence when certain parenting tasks were in demand. She found herself coming home from work and devoting the rest of the night to caring for baby Rachel. The ritual included feeding, bathing, diaper changing, washing dirty diapers, and best of all rock-a-by-baby time. Often Bill was downstairs listening to music. The weekends were even worse.

When Bill wasn't canoeing, he was playing golf with his friends. It seemed it never occurred to him that in a successful marriage both parents are involved. Phyllis' emotional resentment began to escalate. But, according to her upbringing on her dad's side, she kept a stiff upper lip and said little while inwardly steaming with anger. Instead of improving, her home situation got worse.

One time, though, Bill got a full-blown dose of what is involved in being a parent. Phyllis was low on diapers and Rachel was sound asleep.

"Bill," Phyllis told him, "I need to run out to get some diapers. I won't be gone over 30 minutes."

Bill glanced over at Rachel and nonchalantly said, "Sure. Take your time."

When she returned home, Bill was walking the floor trying to comfort Rachel who was exercising her great lungs. "You told me she'd stay asleep for a couple of hours. I've got news for you. You hadn't been gone 10 minutes before she woke up. Not only has she peed, but she has also pooped. The poop messed up her crib sheets!" Bill handed Rachel over to Phyllis. "See if you can get her to stop crying." Phyllis found it hard to keep from laughing as Bill unloaded his diatribe of woes. Later that evening she found the soiled sheet in the dirty clothesbasket. Sandwiched within its folds was one soiled diaper full of poop! Phyllis shook her head and mumbled, "The Lord have mercy!"

Phyllis gave herself a D- when it came to infant breastfeeding! On one occasion she had finished nursing Rachel and placed her sleeping baby in her crib. She then tiptoed over to join Bill who already was fast asleep.

In less than five minutes the air was pierced with strident screams. Phyllis became unglued. Not knowing what else to do for her baby, she joined the chorus, blubbering even louder than her distressed child. Not even Bill Miller could sleep through the rising crescendo.

Rubbing his sleep-crusted eyes, Bill inquired: "What's going on? You're crying. Rachel's crying."

"Bill, Rachel has been crying off and on all day! I'm a total failure as a mother."

Bill said nothing. Instead he slid out of bed and headed to the kitchen. Fifteen minutes later he returned with a bottle of baby formula and stuck it in Phyllis' hands.

"Rachel's hungry and is begging you to feed her," he said.

Tiny Rachel guzzled down the milk. This time when Phyllis laid her down, Rachel slept throughout the night.

Amazed, Phyllis asked Bill, "How did you know she was hungry?"

Bill ran his hands through his hair. "It was just a hunch. Can we get some sleep?"

Phyllis knew her marriage and her emotions were falling apart. What she didn't know was how to put them back together. Once she overcame the initial shock of being a parent and learned some skills, she delighted in her new role. However, she couldn't find any peace of mind in her relationship with Bill.

Somewhere along the way the two of them had developed different philosophies toward marriage. She realized that they should have had deeper discussions prior to getting married on what their expectations and goals would be and their attitude toward having children and being parents. This became a black cloud hovering over their marriage, ready at any moment to create chaos. Her submerged anger toward Bill, never expressed, intensified.

Phyllis thought: *I've achieved great success in my chosen career. However, my fairy tale marriage is in shreds. What went wrong? Two people fall in love, get married, and live happily ever after. I now know that's a pile of malarkey.*

Ways of dealing with personal crisis, learned early in life, are very difficult to change. By the time Rachel was two, Phyllis and Bill realized they'd reached a point of no return. He agreed to move out, and they worked together to make the transition less strenuous on Rachel. With Bill's departure, Phyllis found herself beginning to heal emotionally. She devoted herself to her daughter and to her career, and fortunately had the help of some wonderful caregivers for Rachel.

Phyllis maintained a good relationship with her in-laws, and they were very helpful in helping to care for their grandchild. Rachel worshipped Bill's parents, and the feeling was mutual. Rachel also adored Nana Dot. When Phyllis would be called to work, Nana Dot was there to care for Rachel. On Sundays Nana Dot, the pianist for a small North Georgia church, would sit Rachel by her side as she played the piano. Sometimes, Rachel sat in a carrier near the piano.

Phyllis pushed her failed marriage to the back burner of her mind, aiming to deal with it sometime in the future. Meanwhile, she went full throttle ahead as an OB-GYN doctor. At the same time, the moment she got home and hung up her white coat she switched roles. At home she was Rachel's devoted mother. The moment Phyllis walked through the door, Rachel came running with her tiny hands outstretched. Phyllis swooped her into her arms and covered her with kisses.

At first Rachel couldn't understand why her mom would have to leave home in a hurry. She learned early on that when the phone rang, Mommy would be leaving. Just hearing the ringing phone would cause Rachel to cry. Throwing her arms around her mother she'd beg, "Mommy, Mommy, please don't leave me!"

As Rachel grew older, Phyllis explained to her: "Honey, Mommy is a doctor and sometimes she has to leave to help somebody who is sick. That's the only reason I'll ever leave you. Nana Dot will always stay with you until I get back. Do you understand?"

Rachel hugged Mommy and said, "Mommy loves Rachel. Rachel loves Mommy! Let's play with my clown dolls."

More and more Phyllis found her role as Rachel's mom, coupled with her ever-expanding OB-GYN work, to be most fulfilling, even exhilarating!

One day a mentor of Phyllis' asked, "Don't you ever go out to eat dinner or do something just for fun?"

Phyllis grinned. "What do you mean? I go out all the time. I go to McDonald's or Pizza Hut or Big Boy every week."

Phyllis supported her daughter in many ways., including ballet lessons and attendance at sports activities and even her food choices.

Early on, Rachel became a vegetarian. Phyllis, believing a vegetarian diet was healthy, raised no objections—even when her daughter's tray held a baked potato, creamed potatoes, and French fries!

Rachel was eight when her parents officially divorced. By then, Rachel had visited in the home of friends who had both a father and mother. If she secretly harbored thoughts that one day her mother and father would bury their differences and she'd once again have a family, she never verbalized it. She even told her mother, "Mommy, I like it being just you and me."

For days after the divorce became final, Rachel seemed caught up in her own thoughts, only speaking her innermost thoughts late at night after she had crawled into bed. With tears trickling down her face one night, she confided to one of her clown dolls that Bill's mother made for her, "Daddy and Mommy don't love each other anymore." She stopped long enough to hug her clown doll. "I don't understand why Daddy and Mommy don't love each other." Then she sighed. "Mommy loves me dearly. Mommy needs Rachel. Goodnight, clown doll."

As Phyllis made great advances in her profession, she also relished her role as mom to Rachel, now a budding preteen. Early on, Rachel had a keen interest in anything related to aviation or space. She'd drag Mommy's suitcase into the living room, crawl inside, and cast her eyes toward the nearby airport, visible from their window.

One day Phyllis came home and found a note Rachel had scribbled: "Mom, when I grow up, I want to be a pilot like my Uncle Charles."

When ice skating events were aired on TV, Rachel sat glued to the screen. "Mama," she asked, "Why can't Chattanooga have an ice-skating rink?"

Phyllis answered, "Only large cities have ice skating rinks. Ice skating isn't as popular as football and baseball."

Rachel sighed. "Mama, sometimes in my dreams I'm on a pair of ice skates whirling around in an ice-skating rink doing leaps into the air and creating figure 8s. The crowd goes wild when I make my appearance." Rachel's crest-fallen face broke Phyllis' heart. "Oh, well, so much for dreams."

Phyllis reached for Rachel's hands. "Don't ever let go of your dreams! I was telling a friend about how much you wanted to ice skate and how since you were a toddler you'd taken ballet lessons. As luck would have it, my friend once lived in Atlanta. She told me that Atlanta has a big ice-skating rink and offers ice-skating classes. Would you like for us to go to Atlanta and see what it's all about?"

Rachel struck a pirouette pose as she whirled around and around on her pointed toes. "Would you do that for me, Mama?"

"Honey, I'd like nothing more than to help you live your dream."

Rachel's face glowed. "Mama, you're a dream-maker. When do we leave?"

For several years Phyllis devoted her weekends to helping Rachel successfully participate in ice-skating competitions throughout the Southeast, often with her grandmother in tow. Although she always placed in the top three of every competition and was highly competitive, Rachel recognized she was at a disadvantage when competing with individuals who lived in cities that had skating rinks where they could practice on a daily basis.

Rachel quickly adapted by adding modern dance routines to her repertoire and participating on the dance team at Baylor School in Chattanooga that regularly performed at school sports events. At the same time Rachel continued taking ballet while holding fast to her airplane pilot dream.

While Rachel was a junior in high school, she began taking flying lessons and received her license shortly after beginning her freshman year in college.

Phyllis was a proud parent when Rachel got her wings, but couldn't resist teasing her daughter when she took her mother on as her first passenger: "It's a little hard to trust someone whose diapers you changed."

Rachel winked and cautioned, "Buckle up, Mom. There's no need to worry." Then pretending to be serious, she said, "You've made your funeral arrangements, haven't you?"

Professional
&
Personal Life
1998-2019

Yes, I'll Serve

Phyllis rendered countless volunteer hours at Erlanger Hospital, around Hamilton County, and in the state of Tennessee. Her extra service duties made inroads on her office time with her patients and robbed her of many hours she could have spent with her daughter. Despite the negatives, Phyllis had a deep inner desire to share her God-given talents with others.

After Phyllis served as chief of staff at Erlanger Hospital from 1993–1995, Doctor Rose encouraged her to run for president of the Chattanooga-Hamilton County Medical Society. "If elected," he said, "you'll serve from 1998–1999. You also need to know that we have two committees that come up with a slate of officers and then the members vote. The committees do not discuss their slate of officers with each other. As chairman of one of the committees, I'm asking you to run on my committee's slate as president. Will you accept the nomination?"

Phyllis smiled. "I'm honored you want me to run as president. I'll get back to you as soon as I gather some information on what it entails."

She picked up the phone and called one of her colleagues. "This is Phyllis Miller. Since you served last year as the president of the medical society, I want to ask you what is expected of the person who serves in that office?"

Her colleague rattled off a list that went with the honored position. Then there was a long pause before he said, "You know our committee is nominating another lady physician."

While Phyllis was surprised that she had unknowingly been talking with the chairman of the other committee, she was shocked to learn she would be running against another female doctor.

Phyllis calmly told her colleague, "Thank you for your time. You've been very helpful."

As soon as she hung up, she dialed Doctor Rose. "I can't believe that both committees are planning to run a woman as a nominee to become president! Do you think Chattanooga is ready for this?"

Doctor Rose chuckled. "We see this as a win-win situation. We've never had a choice before. In the past it has always been choosing between two male doctors We're confident Chattanooga-Hamilton County will respond favorably to either of our presidential candidates. Can I count on your being our representative?"

Phyllis agreed to be a candidate and won, serving as president of the Chattanooga-Hamilton Medical Society with distinction for one year. Her desire to learn, share, and improve her profession drove her to extend her service beyond Erlanger and Hamilton County.

After serving for several years as a trustee for the Tennessee Medical Association, she was approached by one of her male colleagues. "Phyllis, it's 2005 and I think you should run to become TMA's first female president."

Phyllis slapped her hands together and frowned. "You've got to be kidding! The good ole boys would have a hissy fit before they'd be replaced by a woman."

"I know," said her colleague. "We know TMA is run by a group we've labeled as having PMS. They're pale, male, and stale!"

Much to the shock of the PMS crowd and to the delight of the more progressive physicians—who were mostly males—Phyllis won the election for the 2005–2006 term, becoming the first female doctor to serve as president of the Tennessee Medical Association.[12]

Claiming Her Heritage

Through the years, Phyllis and her brother Charles held on to their family's original homesite. For years he begged her to let him build her a cabin on the property less than a mile from their childhood home. Phyllis finally agreed, and in 2004 Charles began work on the cabin that for him became a labor of love. During that time Phyllis and Charles often swapped growing-up stories.

On one occasion Phyllis momentarily closed her eyes and when she opened them, tears trickled down her cheeks. "Charles, it would mean so much to me if somehow Mama and Daddy could know that you and I turned out alright."

Charles observed, "Who is to say they don't know? I figure it this way: If anybody has a straight line from the Pearly Gates to earth, it would be Mama."

Phyllis smiled. "We need to find a way to make sure Mama and Daddy are never forgotten. I'm thinking maybe we could give a scholarship in their honor at Polk County High School. Charles, what do you think of that?"

Charles didn't hesitate. "Sis, you're on to something big. Go for it!" He paused. "If I know Phyllis Edwards, she isn't going to stop until a memorial to Mama and Daddy happens."

True to Charles' prediction and after many personal contacts, phone calls, and letters, the Polk County Education Foundation was born. Early on, Phyllis realized that many citizens from Polk County—including people currently living in Polk County and some who once called it home—were eager to participate in the work of the Foundation.

It became an excellent way to honor Polk County's outstanding past leaders while at the same time giving assistance to worthy students seeking to go to college. Each scholarship continues for four years, as long as requirements are met and funds are available. This perpetual fund is supported and sustained by many individuals and organizations. While the majority of the funds support general scholarships, under the umbrella of the Foundation, individuals and families can set up scholarships to honor a loved one.

Phyllis and Charles have set up a named scholarship in memory of their parents. The Arthur T. and Lela B. Edwards scholarship is awarded every four years. Other people have done the same thing while also supporting the general scholarship fund for the Foundation. This has been very gratifying to both Phyllis and Charles.

Phyllis is most grateful for the relationship she has with Charles. She recognizes she had opportunities he did not have. After graduating from high school, she felt free to pursue her dreams, whereas Charles, who graduated two years before Phyllis, felt responsible to stay close to home because of their parents' health at the time.[13]

Recipients of Polk County Education Foundation scholarships

A Troublesome Time

In 2010, Phyllis began serving a five-year term on the board of directors for Erlanger Hospital. She had barely begun her tenure when the CEO was fired due to financial problems. The chairman of the Erlanger board of directors asked Phyllis to chair a search committee to select a new CEO.

After much thought and prayerful consideration, she consented. "Yes, I will. However, I'm concerned that certain groups are going to come down harshly on you for instigating this move."

The search committee, under the leadership of Phyllis, hired a firm whose business was to tackle requests involving personnel changes for large institutions. Phyllis felt strongly that racial bias should not be a factor in the decision. The search firm produced a number of well-qualified, diverse candidates. Charlesetta Woodward, the interim CEO and an African American, was not among them.

"My committee," reported Phyllis, "has hired a firm that has run a national search for our job description. We believe we have found the best CEO candidate that Erlanger currently needs, and we've been diligent not to let racial or gender bias affect our decision."

To one of her committee members Phyllis confided: "I couldn't sleep at night if we caved in on our CEO nominee. My heart and my mind tell me we have made the right choice for what Erlanger needs at this time."

While all the members of the search committee bore stress marks for defending their position, Phyllis took a lot of darts and incurred some lingering scars—including some doctors who quit speaking to her. But, while she made some enemies, she also cemented deep relationships with other board members and members of the medical community.

One of the doctors who was so vocal in opposition to the committee's decision came up to Phyllis after the meeting and said, "Although I don't agree with your decision, I do respect you and the committee and the process and I will work with the new person."

Meanwhile, the work at Erlanger returned to its usual chaotic pace. And, in the midst of her professional duties, Phyllis found her thoughts often turning to Polk County.

Climbing Mount Kilimanjaro

In 2009, as president of the Tennessee Medical Association, Phyllis had just completed the most exhilarating stint of her professional career. For two years she felt as if she'd been in an active whirlwind. She'd wake each morning to emails needing a response. Her duties involved one or two trips to Nashville each week in addition to traveling across the state.

Her weekends were often spent going to other nearby states' annual meetings as a guest, and twice each year she attended the American Medical Association meetings. Sandwiched between her demanding TMA schedule, Phyllis made what time she could for her daughter and her private OB-GYN practice.

Letting go a big sigh, Phyllis said to one of her associates, "Now that I've finished my demanding yet wonderful role as TMA president, what am I going to do with myself?" Before her friend could offer a suggestion, Phyllis added, "I know what I'll do: I'll climb Mount Kilimanjaro!"

Her friend, in complete shock, scratched the base of his neck. "You're joking aren't you, Phyllis?"

Phyllis leaned back in her desk chair. "Nope. I'm dead serious. Stand by as I make a call to the Wilderness Medical Society to make a reservation for my friend Jackie and me."

After confirming her reservation, Phyllis began a strenuous workout program. She hired a personal trainer, hiked, rode her bicycle, and could be seem in the late evenings plodding up and down the twists and turns leading to her house, with a heavy-laden backpack astraddle her back. Upon reaching home, Phyllis would remove her backpack and head for the refrigerator for some bottled water. As she plopped onto her easy chair, her dog Timber would made a flying leap onto her lap.

As Phyllis began caressing Timber's ears, she expelled a heavy sigh. "Timber, I think I should have decided to climb Mount Kilimanjaro when I was 40 instead of 60. What do you think?"

Timber cocked his head to one side, pretending to be sympathetic while at the same time fasting his eyes on his empty doggie bowl. Phyllis chuckled as she got up and filled his bowl. While Timber wolfed down his dog food, Phyllis thought, *Oh, what I'd give to sink my teeth into a juicy steak. . . . I guess I'd better settle for a tossed tuna salad.*

Day after day, week after week, and month after month there was no let-up in Phyllis' fitness schedule. One day a phone call from Jackie sent Phyllis reeling.

"Phyllis," said Jackie, "You'll have to get yourself another partner. I won't be able to make the trip with you to Mount Kilimanjaro!"

Phyllis thanked Jackie for letting her know her plans had been changed and hung up the phone. But then she muttered to herself, "Oh, no! Just when I thought everything was going well, things are starting to fall apart."

She began racking her brain trying to come up with a replacement for Jackie. Still carrying on a conversation with herself, Phyllis allowed that her daughter Rachel was the only physically fit person she knew who could step in at such a late date.

Phyllis picked up the phone and dialed Rachel.

"Hello, Mom," said Rachel. "How are you?"

Phyllis released a heavy sigh. "Rachel, you're not going to believe this. A few minutes ago, Jackie called and told me she can't go with me to Kilimanjaro." Her voice broke. "What on earth will I do without a partner?"

Rachel's voice sounded strong. "Mom, calm down. Let's think this problem through. How long will you be gone?"

Phyllis answered, "Seven or eight days at the most. The climb up Kilimanjaro is only for a few days. You don't think . . .?"

"Gee whiz, Mom. You don't give me a choice. There's no way I'm going to let my super-disoriented mom climb a mountain without someone who knows her well. I can see you now meandering from the main group and screaming for help. It's settled. I'm going to climb Mount Kilimanjaro with you."

Phyllis said, "Thanks, Rachel. You're like a knighted warrior astride a white stallion, racing to my rescue."

The time for preparing for the arduous trip passed quickly. Rachel and her husband Robbie arrived at Phyllis' house on January 19, 2010, a little after 4:00 a.m. Timber, sensing something ominous was about to happen, went berserk, running high speed in circles and clamoring for attention from everyone. Phyllis and Rachel left Chattanooga on a shuttle bus for Atlanta.

Upon arriving at the airport, Phyllis zipped through the passport area. It wasn't so pleasant for Rachel, however, as her passport visa read Rachel Miller and her ticket read Rachel Miller Tester. She was sent to the end of the line.

Meanwhile, Phyllis began wrestling with getting past the security check lane. Her carry-on bag and purse were strung upside down around her neck. Jutting out of her open purse were several papers looking as if they might take flight any moment. Phyllis glanced over to where Rachel was standing and found her grinning from ear to ear.

The security guard instructed, "Open your duffle bag."

When Phyllis unzipped her duffle bag, one of her tennis shoes sailed away, allowing the guard to view her inept packing skills.

The guard hastily said, "Never mind. Zip your duffle bag and retrieve your carry-on items."

Soon Rachel had her visa permit and joined Phyllis at the boarding area.

Phyllis inquired, "What did you find so funny about my going through the security check point?"

"I love you, Mom, but let's face it: being organized is not one of your best traits! It seems unreal to me that someone can be so adept in the operating room and at delivering babies and at the same time be unable to navigate their way through a security check point. Give me your carry-on bag. Our flight for Newark, New Jersey, will soon be loading."

After a four-hour snow delay in Newark, Phyllis and Rachel had to wait for their plane to be de-iced before they could leave for Amsterdam. During their eight-hour KLM flight to Kilimanjaro, a guide shared with them some historical data about the mountain.

"Mount Kilimanjaro, at 19,336 feet, is the highest peak on the continent of Africa, and it's the tallest free-standing mountain in the world when measured from the base on which it sits. The good news for you is that despite its size, Kili is one of the world's most accessible summits. Kili is a giant strato-volcano that began forming a million years ago. Don't let that bother you. The last time Kili erupted was 360,000 years ago!"

The plane landed at the Kilimanjaro Airport on January 21 at 8:30 p.m. Phyllis and Rachel were immediately swamped by what seemed like a hundred people wanting to help them. They juggled their way to join the passport line, only to be told later that they needed to first visit the visa line. So, they regrouped and joined the winding visa line. No one seemed to be in a hurry to issue visa passes.

When at last all their legal work had been completed, they received a rousing welcome from their tour guides before boarding a rickety bus for Arumeru Lodge, 15 or 20 miles from the airport.

After checking out their temporary living quarters, Rachel said, "Mom, can you believe it? We don't have air conditioning or television."

Phyllis grinned. "Try not to get too upset. When I was a youngster, we had no electricity." She waved her hands. "That meant no indoor plumbing, electric lights, air conditioning, or television."

As her eyes danced with mischief, Rachel pleaded: "Please, Mom. No more Polk County stories! I suppose I can survive without television for a week." She paused before adding, "Help me unpack our gear."

If Phyllis qualifies as Madam Disorganized in all unofficial matters, then Rachel seems to qualify as Ms. Overly Organized.

Rachel seemed pleased with the rustic living quarters until she reached inside a basket containing body wash. Much to her chagrin, a slithering lizard moved quickly to escape being captured. She screamed but Phyllis told her to think nothing of it, that lizards are our friends.

"But, Mom," said Rachel, "I can't help myself."

Phyllis looked on as her daughter went on a bug-killing mission, then later heard Rachel mutter as she began organizing her mother's duffle bag, "Mom is so messy."

Before beginning their official climb up Mount Kilimanjaro, Phyllis and Rachel visited Cradle of Love, an orphanage for children age two or younger who were born in the jungle with no medical personnel in attendance. Cradle of Love is operated by an American woman with ties to the Seventh Day Adventist Church.

The lady told her visitors, "Come see our triplets. Originally, they were quadruplets, but one died. And their mother died in childbirth from hemorrhage. Their daddy visits them every day and when they get big enough, he'll take them home with him." She paused before saying, "Most of our children will eventually go back to their families or become adopted. A few of them will end up in an institution for older children."

During their brief visit at the orphanage a little boy continuously hugged Phyllis, even after she told him she had to leave. Every time she tried to break loose, he'd respond with huge tears streaming down his face. Before Phyllis and Rachel left the orphanage, they spent some time playing with a little boy who laughed the entire time they were there.

Back at the lodge Phyllis whispered to Rachel, "Most of our group is either your age or slightly older. Suddenly I feel old—very old!"

They left Arumeru Lodge the following morning for Kilimanjaro National Park to register for their climb. That afternoon they began the first leg of their journey up the mountain.

Phyllis wrote in her diary: "Today we hiked to the Shira Plateau, 11,500 feet. This is only the first day of our climb, and the limits of my endurance have already been severely tested. The climb today was grueling! We arrived at our campsite dog-tired, dirty, hungry, and sleepy! The best part was finding that our 70-member support team, all Tanzanians, had gone before us and had our tents, portable toilets, food, etc. all in place."

Toward the end of their first day up the mountain both Rachel and Phyllis became sick. A member of their tour group, a follower of the practice known as Reiki, insisted on helping them. Feeling she could pass healing energy from the palms of her hands to encourage emotional or physical healing, she began massaging Phyllis' head. When she started in on her bone-tired feet, Phyllis thanked her and told her she'd had enough.

Both Phyllis and Rachel were awake most of the night, making sure each other was okay and breathing. Rachel hugged Phyllis and encouraged her. "Mom, try to get some sleep. We need to be rested for tomorrow. Let's take this climb one day at a time."

Soon Phyllis fell asleep with the guide's command words "pole, pole" (go slowly, slowly) ringing in her ears. In a couple of hours she awoke, shivering from the plunging temperature and unable to go back to sleep.

On day two the tour group reached an altitude of 12,000 feet. That night Rachel and Phyllis were crawling into their sleeping bags when both of them were hit by an incessant urge to pee. The more they tried to put their urge on hold, the stronger the urge became.

The tent housing the bathroom facilities was some distance from their personal tent, so they crawled into their leggings, grabbed their headgear, and checked to make sure their lantern lights were working. When they stepped outside the tent, they began to shiver. It was bitter cold, and the skyline was inky black. They stumbled toward the necessities tent.

As usual, Phyllis had a problem: her helmet was tilted and caused her headlight to beam into the tents where other people were sleeping. The more she tried to adjust her helmet, the worse the situation became. Finally, Phyllis and Rachel reached their destination and took care of their business. Then Rachel adjusted her mother's helmet, and the two of them returned to their tent.

Once they were in their sleeping bags, Rachel warned Phyllis: "When I get home, I'm going to sue you for false advertising about this trip!"

Day three found Phyllis clawing her way straight up the Barranco rock wall to an elevation of 13,000 feet. After stopping for a short snack, the climbers resumed their trek through two more valleys. By now Phyllis had resigned herself to bringing up the rear, with constant enforcement messages from Rachel.

As she stumbled into her cold tent that night at Barranco Camp, Phyllis told Rachel: "Every muscle in my body is crying out for help!" Before nose-diving into her sleeping bag, she whispered, "Rachel, I'm not a quitter, but then again I'm not crazy. Honey, I'm . . ." She never finished what she was saying. Phyllis had fallen into a deep sleep.

Rachel roused Phyllis a few hours later. Although she felt dreadful, Phyllis forced herself to eat a light breakfast before joining her fellow climbers as they hiked to Barafu Camp (15,000 feet). The trek on Summit night was straight up, rocky, and dark. Adjusting her headlight and wobbling one step at the time, Phyllis made a last-ditch effort. Rachel hovered close behind, stoking her mom with high-energy jellybeans.

By the time Phyllis and Rachel reached an altitude of 17,000 feet they were both constantly upchucking and dizzy-headed. Phyllis begged Busto, one of their guides, "Please let me sit here on this rock and get some sleep."

Busto's eyes grew large. He exclaimed, "No! No! We must not stop."

Rachel told the guide, "It is no longer safe for my mother and me to keep climbing. We can go no further."

"Okay," said Busto, "then I'll guide you safely back to Camp Barafu."

They slowly began their descent, upchucking with almost every step they took. Their trip down to Barafu was most difficult. Upon reaching Camp Barafu, Phyllis and Rachel, with the help of their guide, cast off their backpacks and boots and crawled into their sleeping bags. They slept for many hours. By the time they awoke, the summit climbers had returned. After eating a hearty meal with the returning climbers, Phyllis and Rachel continued their trek down Mount Kilimanjaro.

Once they were back at the Arumeru River Lodge, they spent the night repacking their bags. Rachel would soon be leaving for home, but Phyllis had signed on with Wilderness Medicine for an African safari. The first thing Rachel wrote in her diary after separating from her mom was "I miss Mom. I really miss my Mom!"[14]

Phyllis and Rachel on their trip to Mount Kilimanjaro

Earthquake Doctoring

It was 2010 and Phyllis, who always exuded optimism and dedication to her medical profession, was struggling. Swamped by bureaucratic demands, not to mention some personal problems, she felt jaded.

As she contemplated her plight, her thoughts turned to Dr. Mitch Mutter, one of Chattanooga's outstanding cardiologists who in 1995 had spearheaded the formation of the Children's Nutrition Program in Haiti. Phyllis tapped her fingers on her cluttered desk. *I know what I'll do! I'll call Doctor Mutter and volunteer to go on one of his trips to Haiti. Going on a mission trip to a country in desperate need of medical help … Hmm, that should snap me out of my pity spell.*

Phyllis contacted Doctor Mutter, who was happy to have her join his team on their next trip to Leogane, 30 miles south of Haiti's capital city of Port-au-Prince.

Everything was falling in place for the trip to Haiti when the National Television Service exploded with news that a 7.0 earthquake had landed near Port-au-Prince, where 70 percent of its people live below the poverty level and whose building infrastructures wouldn't stand a ghost of a chance of surviving.

Doctor Mutter called a meeting of the Haiti team, saying, "This devastating 7.0 earthquake forces us to change our plans." He wiped the tears falling down his cheeks. "However, it is most imperative that we go to Haiti and do what we can to help them survive this dreadful carnage. We'll fly from Chattanooga to Port-au-Prince. Brace yourself." The brave doctor wrung his hands. "There is no way I can prepare myself or you for what lies ahead."

Sensing the unbelievable chaos that would soon confront them revived Phyllis' sagging spirits, reminding her of why she had originally become a doctor. Her adrenalin was running high when their plane flew over the city of Port-au-Prince. As far as her eyes could travel, she saw capsized buildings and a mass of people roaming through mounds of rubbish. But that was not all Phyllis saw. Moored in the nearby waters of Port-au-Prince was a host of medical ships.

Phyllis nudged one of her companions. "This is a spine-tingling sight. We're part of an international effort to help Haitians survive this great tragedy."

Once their plane landed, a driver in a dilapidated jeep was waiting to transfer them and their meager supplies to their destination in Leogane. The road leading from Port-au-Prince to Leogane, even in its better days, had been a hazard in the making. Now the driver was forced to skirt around huge potholes and mounds of debris. Missing all the potholes was impossible. Every time the driver hit a pothole, Phyllis and her friends grabbed each other to keep from exiting through the open jeep frame.

Upon their arrival in Leogane, they found the hospital belonging to the city totally obliterated. Doctor Mutter 's jaw dropped. "It's for sure we won't be using the hospital!"

Likewise, the nearby nursing school had been closed. However, they soon discovered that someone had converted the building where the nursing students lived into a medical facility. The nursing students were living in tents on the lawn where the head of the nursing school lived.

"We're fortunate," said Doctor Mutter, "that our team has the use of a house belonging to Bill Gates that we can use for sleeping and eating." Gazing at the long line awaiting them, Doctor Mutter told the group, "We need to begin seeing patients before we're totally engulfed in darkness." Pointing to a nearby table he said, "We'll use this table for our operations."

It was 10:00 p.m. and Phyllis and a colleague were preforming a C-section when they found themselves without lights. "Quick!' Phyllis said, "Someone alert the Japanese that we need them to turn the lights back on so we can finish our surgery."

While the Japanese were manning the electrical generator, Phyllis whispered to her colleague, "Our chances of success seem slim. I hope we can save both the mother and her baby."

Phyllis and her colleague labored intensely over their patient. When they delivered the baby, it barely had a heartbeat. The team's nurse anesthetist lost no time responding. After dispensing oxygen to the baby, he then gave oxygen to the mother.

The baby responded extremely well to the resuscitation efforts. In a couple of hours Phyllis and her cohorts felt it was safe for them to get some sleep. Thus, during the wee hours of dawn and after a fulfilling yet grueling first day in Haiti, Phyllis sought her cot for some much-needed sleep. Alas! The mournful wails from the masses of desperate Haitians made sleep impossible.

The next morning Phyllis was amazed to find the baby, who began life struggling for breath, alert, dressed in an adorable outfit and ready to go home. Phyllis remarked, "These Haitians are so resilient. Give them a few hours and they snap back from the jaws of death. I admire their tenacity to survive."

A young pregnant girl, having walked a long distance, groped her way to the treatment station. Suspecting she had a contagious disease, Phyllis sent her to the courtyard where an infectious disease doctor confirmed she had malaria. The girl was given the appropriate medicines and sent home. Considering the limited treatment time and the defunct facility, this was the best Phyllis and her team could do. They could only hope her body responded well to the medication they gave her, for there was no time for follow-ups and no option of hospitalization.

Turning to one of her colleagues Phyllis added, "Wow! Even with our meager facilities and equipment, we have immediate access to colleagues in other specialties! Back home, in order to help her I would have had to make a phone call to get authorization from insurance companies. After that she'd have go to another office, probably far away, for consultation."

By the middle of their week in Haiti the group gained access to a tent and their own generator. Phyllis discovered that the night vigil belonged solely to her, one nurse, and a student nurse. One of the doctors, before leaving, tossed Phyllis the keys to the generator. He had no sooner left than a pregnant patient and her husband arrived. Phyllis turned on the generator and escorted them to a bed.

Phyllis was able to interpret enough of their conversation to realize there was a high risk that the mother would hemorrhage. Phyllis knew that she had no quick access to perform surgery or to give a blood transfusion. While anxiously watching for any complications, she and her two helpers dined on tuna fish sandwiches in a corner adjacent to the woman in labor as they waited for nature to take its course.

In due time the woman delivered a beautiful baby with no complicating issues. As the couple left to return home, Phyllis asked, "Who is taking care of your other children?"

The husband, visibly shaken, said, "Since the earthquake destroyed our house, we huddle together under a small tarp. Our neighbor, in the tarp next to ours, is taking care of our two sons."

One day Phyllis eyed a young mother plodding her way toward the clinic. She had a cast on her right leg and was hoisting an infant on her waist. Holding her hand against her rapid beating heart, she said, "I've come a long way to have my cast taken off." With desperation clouding her vision she implored, "Can someone help my baby?"

Phyllis, realizing the infant was very ill, called for a pediatrician who took one look at the infant and said, "The baby is extremely dehydrated and will die if she doesn't get immediate help." The doctors went to work, and in a few hours the baby and mother left the clinic and went back to wherever they lived.[15]

Phyllis with the Tester family at her grandson Mac's christening

Phygi and Her Grandchildren

Grandmothers, regardless of their age, education, or social standing are very special in a family's hierarchy, leaving a lasting impression on their grandchildren. Sometimes the impressions left by grandmothers can be crippling. However, grandmothers are more often the heroic enablers for their grandchildren.

Newspaper columnist Doug Larson quipped, "Few things are more delightful than having grandchildren fighting over your lap."

An unknown author said, "Grandmas hold our tiny hands for just a little while, but our hearts forever."

Most grandchildren have a special name for their grandmother. Doctor Phyllis Miller is no exception. To her grandsons, Jaxson and Mac, she is Phygi.

When he was born in 2011, Jaxson caused quite a stir in the Miller-Tester households. With big tears in her eyes, Rachel told her mother when he was about two weeks old, "Mom, two weeks ago my life was normal. Now everything is upside down."

Phyllis told her, "I understand how you feel. You'll find that Jaxson gradually grows on you and one day you'll realize he has your heart."

Several months later Phyllis observed Rachel looking at him with so much love in her eyes and she commented, "I believe he now has your heart, doesn't he?"

Rachel replied, "Yes, he does. I really can't imagine life without Jaxson. He's such a bundle of love."

For several years there was only Jaxson, so Phyllis had some special moments with him. When he was two or three, she went with his family on a beach trip.

One morning when Jaxson joined Phyllis on the balcony of their condo as she sipped her morning coffee, he asked, "Phygi, do you have a man?"

Phyllis was puzzled by what he said and asked him to say it again. He repeated what he had said before. When she finally understood what he was asking, she told him, "No, I don't."

Jaxson assured her, "Phygi, I'll be your man."

Phyllis responded, "Jaxson, it's okay that I don't have a man. Please don't worry about Phygi."

It's a long drive from Chattanooga to Phyllis' cabin in Polk County, Tennessee. On one trip there, around the time of Jaxson's preschool St. Patrick's Day activities, Phygi conjured up ways to keep Jaxson entertained.

When they entered the terrain surrounded by mountains, Phygi warned, "Watch out for bears. Let me know if you spot one."

In a few minutes Jaxson observed, "Phygi, I don't see any bears, but the woods are full of leprechauns. They're all green and you can't see them, but I do!'

After arriving at the cabin that is encircled by a thick forest of trees and babbling brooks, Phyllis summoned, "Jaxson, let's go on a bear hunt." She handed him a bag of popcorn and told him, "The bears are probably hungry and would like something to eat."

Jaxson, holding tightly to Phygi's hand, expected any minute to see a huge black bear peeping up at them from the tall trees or bushes. After several minutes of searching he said, "Phygi, the bears are hiding from us. Why don't they come out?"

"The bears are hiding because they're afraid of us. Let's leave behind a trail of popcorn. Probably as soon as we go back to the cabin they'll come out."

When they got back to the cabin Phygi sat down in the rocking chair owned by her mother. "Jaxson," she said, "climb onto my lap and let me read you a story."

Creak, creak went the rocker. By the time Phygi had read the story through a second time, Jaxson was sound asleep. Phygi gently laid him on the couch and, after covering him with a blanket, curled up beside him and also took a nap.

It's a long drive from Chattanooga to Phyllis' cabin in Polk County, Tennessee. Mac enjoy going home with Phygi. With their grandmother in tow, they like to explore a storage closet adjacent to the basement. Phygi shares with them toys that once belonged to their mother. When they find a toy they like, Phygi cleans it up so they can play with it.

Jaxson and Mac seem to prefer the older toys over newly acquired ones. Since their mom is a pilot and their dad is in the air ambulance industry, their favorite toy is an ambulance that once belonged to their mom. Mac makes the shrill, nerve-rattling sound of an approaching ambulance and rushes his patients to the nearest hospital. He repeats this same action over and over. The boys also have a whole fleet of airplanes and helicopters in their toy collection.

During his early development and pre-walking months, Mac spent a lot of time exercising his lungs! Left in the church nursery with people he didn't know, he wouldn't stop crying until his parents or Phygi came to rescue him. His dislike of strange places and people continued into his preschool years. One day when Phygi was driving the boys home, she listened in on their backseat conversation.

Mac said, "I don't like church."

Jaxson spoke up. "Mac, church is where we learn about God, Jesus, and the Bible."

Mac was adamant. "I don't like church!"

While Mac doesn't like going to church, he does enjoy going to Phygi's house. He arrives there squealing and with his arms open wide and a big smile on his face. He isn't there long before he finds Timber. "Yip Yip!" goes Timber as he bounces over to greet Mac. The two tussle and nuzzle until Timber drops his favorite ball at Mac's feet and a game of catch ensues.

Jaxson also likes to play ball. Now at age eight, he is into sports. Phygi likes attending his Little League baseball games where he plays shortstop. She'd never admit it to anyone, but surely everyone knows her grandson is the best player on the team and by far the most handsome, loving kid in the universe.

For most of her life Phyllis has been known to play by the rules. Even those who disagree with her professional opinions have applauded her sense of fair play. However, there seems to be something she has acquired in her role as a grandmother that defies logic.

When caught red-handed breaking the law, Phyllis' first reaction was that it wasn't what it seemed to be. In other words, she was innocent. Lately she's admitting guilt but now tweets, "Grandmothers don't have to abide by the rules."

Some wag added, "Tell that to your local policeman. ... On the other hand, never mind. With your infectious smile and good looks, he'd probably exonerate you. Case dismissed!"

Charles and Phyllis

Phyllis and Rachel

A 72-Hour Retirement

Phyllis, after 40-plus years as an OB-GYN doctor, in 2017 began exploring her options for the future. She confided to a friend, "My grandsons are only going to be young for a brief span of time. I believe now is the perfect time for me to enjoy doing things with them and at the same time giving my daughter some breathing room in their upbringing."

Her friend responded, "That's certainly true. However, I can't imagine you giving up your practice completely or removing yourself from having a platform to speak out on medical issues dear to your heart. Maybe you can become a part-time retiree."

Phyllis wrinkled her brow as she said, "I've observed too many doctors who chose, unwisely, to continue to operate on patients beyond their prime. I'm determined not to follow that route."

In her semi-retirement mode Phyllis reluctantly gave up her scalpel but continues to work two days every week. She also applied for and was appointed to a position on the Tennessee Board of Medical examiners. Phyllis enjoys going to Nashville for meetings with the board and finds her interactions with this group to be a challenge she welcomes.

Phyllis' daughter Rachel and her husband Robbie jokingly say, "Mom retired for 72 hours!"

Now, with a slower-paced life, Phyllis has the time to pursue outside interests and to spend more time with friends and family.

Even before Phyllis had entered the first grade, she enjoyed tinkering with art projects. Her creativity was limited by a lack of art supplies, however, and schools didn't consider art as part of the core curriculum. In her semi-retirement mode, Phyllis is taking art lessons and honing her skills.

She also delights in traveling to distant lands, reuniting with Polk County folks, getting to know more intimately her brother Charles and his family, and bonding with the members of First Baptist Church of Chattanooga—especially those in the Waters Sunday school class.

And, you can't be around Phyllis long before you discover that her family has priority status, especially Rachel and Robbie and their sons Jaxson and Mac.

Epilogue

"Each of our lives," says Phyllis, "consists of positive and negative experiences. For me the many positive and exhilarating people and events I've been given far outweigh the negatives I've encountered."

Although Phyllis Edwards Miller has, from time to time, been confronted with problems that could have stymied her extraordinary persona and career, she has defiantly refused to let any of them define her personally or professionally. When life has tossed her a lemon, she has managed to turn it into lemonade!

Growing up in the hinterlands of Polk County without modern conveniences, Phyllis early on realized that getting a good education was her ticket to fulfilling her dream of becoming a doctor. Not even the death of her parents, just prior to her finishing high school, caused her to lessen her quest. Earning a scholarship to Tennessee Tech, she pressed onward until the coveted letter of her acceptance into the University of Tennessee's medical school became a reality.

While interning at Baptist Hospital in Memphis, Phyllis was denied an appointment she deserved by a bigoted doctor overseer. She immediately turned her attention to Erlanger Hospital in Chattanooga, where she made historic medical contributions.

Phyllis had the unpleasant task of dealing with a miscarriage and an unsympathetic spouse. Unwilling to believe her marriage was flawed, she then had a successful pregnancy, hoping this would end their marital woes. Seven years later Phyllis had to admit that not all marriages, including hers, were destined to have a "happy ever after" motif.

Those experiences had the potential to do her in at a time when her medical career was rapidly growing. However, refusing to allow a failed relationship to spell her doom, Phyllis redoubled her professional energies while at the same time devoting quality time to her adoring daughter, Rachel.

As Phyllis reflects on her productive life she says, "I'm forever grateful for the loving, caring parents and the community that succored me during my formative years."

As a child, Phyllis and her brother Charles couldn't wait to leave their meager homestead behind. In their later years they've joined with many others to assure there will always be an educational legacy for students in Polk County's schools, while at the same time honoring the memory of their parents and other Polk

County pioneers. Phyllis cherishes memories of bygone days and delights in sharing yesterday moments with her grandchildren.

The brother she sparred with as a child has become, in her senior years, a rock she frequently leans on. Phyllis says, "I believe our parents are looking down from above, wiping their brows and breathing a sigh of relief that we didn't end up in Sing Sing Prison!"

One of the trademarks of Phyllis Miller, M.D., has been her commitment to sharing. Throughout her long professional tenure Phyllis has been called upon to give, without remuneration, of her expertise. She has never failed to respond.

One thing is certain: The future of Dr. Phyllis Edwards Miller will always be full of concrete acts and endearing friendships—some old, some new, and some yet to be formed. Phyllis, whose capable, loving concern for her peers and patients is well documented, will continue being involved in medicine, but at a reduced level. She's in the process of planning for another stint as an instructor in Erlanger's teaching program for young adults.

Recalling her experiences in Haiti, Phyllis says, "I'd welcome the challenge to become engaged in elevating the medical care of citizens living in a far-flung outpost of the world. Meanwhile, I'm very much aware that within the United States. many patients fall through the cracks. I'll continue to volunteer as I have for many years, in whatever way I can in our community. Patients repay me tenfold when I see the gratitude etched on their faces."

Whether in the realm of family, medicine, church, or friends, Phyllis is committed to lasting relationships, expressing gratitude in specific ways and being committed to professional excellence.

There is another side of Phyllis that is equally vibrant. Phyllis enjoys having fun! She says, "The most fun I have is with my grandchildren, but beyond that I'm enjoying having time for old friendships as well as forming new ones whether by visiting and enjoying a good meal or occasionally with a fun game of golf or a nature hike. In my latter days I'm enjoying expressing myself through art. I find it immensely enjoyable and at times frustrating."

Phyllis adds, "I love traveling and plan to continue to indulge myself in some adventuresome trips. One of the things I treasure most is getting away to my cabin and the land of my childhood."

In response to Phyllis' adventure plans, thoughm her friends hope she stays off the grass and never, never plans to go hiking on Mount Kilimanjaro!

Notes

[1]"Bennie and I continued to be lifetime friends, although we pursued different paths. Bennie never had any desire to continue her education. She married David Nicholson soon after high school. They settled in Ocoee adjacent to her childhood home and raised their family there. We did not see each other often, but when we did it was as if we had never been apart. I remember sitting on her front porch talking and drinking coffee. Bennie developed Alzheimer's and died in 2019.

"Pam lived her adult life in Florida and was a very successful teacher. She never married and had a sad life in a lot of ways. She died at age 50 of a rare genetic disease that was discovered when she developed lung issues in her 40s."

[2]"Mrs. Crouch made classroom learning a challenge. By sharing her home and personal television with us, she enhanced our view of a world bigger than ourselves. Perhaps, best of all, Mrs. Crouch had a sense of humor and was able to remember some of the foolish, inane things she also had done when she was our age.

"I find Mrs. Crouch is typical of millions of teachers throughout the United States. To enhance student progress, they go the extra mile in explaining and often spending their own money for supplies and keeping alive their 'I once was a child' memories."

[3]"When my parents died, I remember thinking, 'I will never love again. I'm not ever going to hurt like this again.' Today I realize this is not a healthy reaction. Through much soul-searching and counseling I have been able to overcome this to a great extent. Although I have many friends, I still have difficulty getting beyond a certain point. This affected my marriage, my relationship with my daughter, and my ability to develop meaningful relationships with others. On the positive side, my unhealthy conclusion on loving again has allowed me to buckle down and with laser vision pursue my professional goals.

"This chapter brings out the most painful event of my entire life. Although many other memories are fuzzy and hard for me to recall, I remember the details of my mother's death with great clarity. It has defined me in many ways. It still saddens me greatly to think of the hard life she had and the unfairness of having her life cut short at age 59. My dad's death a few months later was not as shocking, but still very sad. When Dad died, I was still numb over Mom's death and completely empty of feelings."

[4]"My trip to Vanderbilt was a mountaintop experience for me. It made me yearn to be a part of the medical world. It offset any negative reactions I received about my desires. I'm sure the adults looking at my situation were thinking of the odds not being in my favor as far as achieving my goal. Deep down, their attitudes just fueled my desire to prove them wrong. I said to myself, 'I'll show them!'"

[5]"Education was always important for my family. My grandmother was a teacher. My father valued education. His mother had sent him to boarding school in Maryville,

Tennessee. His daddy died when he was nine and his mother raised him and his three younger brothers. There were many of my cousins older than I who went to college, including my Uncle Harle's son."

[6]"Although my job was basically that of a dishwasher, I relished handling the petri dishes with agar that were used for growing bacteria and conducting experiments in the biology class."

[7]"I was mortified over missing the test. If I had not been allowed to take the test, I would have flunked chemistry and therefore probably not continued in pre-med."

[8]"Time and again when I find myself in a situation where I feel insecure, I return to Doctor Kirkland's statement, 'If you can dissect a cadaver, surely you can pour a cup of tea.'"

[9]"My experiences at St. Jude Hospital are some of the highlights of my entire medical career. I was exposed to amazing doctors and scientists from all over the world, and I learned so much from them."

[10]"There is nothing more amazing than the birth of a baby! Only the word miracle can adequately describe what happens from the moment a baby is conceived until it emerges from its mother's body."

[11]"Doctor Howard was sensitive to the fact that residents were usually tight on money. Rather than doing something overtly, she would masquerade her money gifts with what seemed like a flippant act. As resident doctors, we went to health department clinics scattered over a wide area to see patients.

"One day she called me to her office and gave me a check amounting to $800 and told me it was for gas money for driving to the clinics. I said, 'Oh, no, Doctor Howard, I haven't spent that much on gas, maybe $80.00.' She smiled and said, 'Keep it.' Slowly it dawned on me she was giving me a gift and was simply labeling it as gas money! Throughout her tenure at Erlanger this type of gift-giving occurred often to resident doctors.

"Doctor Howard was an amazing teacher. I feel I learned as much in those six months I spent under her as I did in the rest of my residency. She instilled in us a strong work ethic and that our patient always came first."

[12]"I had a good term and made some great friends across the state. Part of my duties was to visit other state medical societies as their guest at their annual meetings. By virtue of my position, I was automatically a delegate to the American Medical Association (AMA) and attended their annual meetings. This brought me into direct contact with America's dominant movers and shakers in medicine.

"Serving as president of the Tennessee Medical Association represents the pinnacle of my activities outside my practice. I'm pleased with how progressive the TMA has become, with more women and minorities being involved in leadership roles.

"Most of the things we doctors get credit or blame for is part of a team effort. We could never do what we do without the invaluable help of a lot of people, especially the nurses. I'd like to also pay tribute to an amazing person, namely Rae Bond, executive director of our medical society, who quietly and without a lot of credit makes things happen."

[13]The Polk County Education Foundation, now in its 16th year, awarded its first scholarship in 2004. Phyllis served as the Foundation's president from 2004–2019, and was named president emeritus in 2019. As of May, 2019, the Foundation had awarded 33 scholarships.

[14]"Rachel and I both were happy to have Kilimanjaro behind us. We considered it a victory that we ascended to 17,000 feet! For us, the trek was extremely difficult and not one bit enjoyable. This is by far the most difficult thing I've ever done.

"The best thing that came out of my climb up Kilimanjaro was the bonding Rachel and I experienced. For a while she became the parent and I became the child. Without Rachel, I would have had to turn back far earlier than I did. She's much more organized than I. At night time she'd come over to my side of the tent and help me find things—such as my toothbrush. When I'd fall behind, she'd stay with me rather than going on with those in her age group. On the last leg of our trip when I was barely able to put one foot in front of the other, she was behind me encouraging me and feeding me high-energy jellybeans!"

[15]"When you're working in an area ravaged by an unrelenting earthquake, normal procedures of follow-up visits aren't considered. You are flooded with so many demands, you're forced to do what you can and not to worry about things beyond your control.

"We were constantly denied a good night's sleep. Earthquake aftershocks—which seemed to always happen during the twilight hours—frightened the masses, sending them into the streets mournfully begging for God's mercy. The cries of the people were accompanied by panic-stricken dogs and crowing roosters.

"This experience was life-changing for me. It happened at a time when I was burned out personally and professionally. It gave me a new perspective. I realized how tiny my problems were compared to what those people were experiencing. In my career I had become frustrated with medicine-insurance rules, administrative hassles. In Haiti we just practiced basic medicine, reminding me of how much fun medicine can be. When the week was up, I was exhausted! On Friday night I thought, 'If something happens and we don't get to go home tomorrow, I think I will just have a nervous breakdown!'"

Haiti medical mission memories, 2010
(above) A valued colleague;
(right) A recovered patient

Appendix: Medical Memories

When I was a medical student at John Gaston Hospital in Memphis, a very young black girl arrived at the clinic in agonizing pain and with a dead fetus dangling from her womb. The girl was the victim of an illegal, back-alley abortion. I edged my way closer as the male resident doctor, his face red with anger, tied a small weight to the leg of the dead fetus to hasten its passage.

"Why are you doing that?" I asked.

The resident responded: "If we're going to be able to save our patient's life, we must completely remove all of the fetus as quickly as possible. Some quack, who calls himself a doctor, has killed the fetus and at the same time put this terrified little girl's life in jeopardy."

I stood entranced as the doctor worked laboriously to save the life of his patient. In the end we lost her. As soon as I got home, I telephoned Dana. "I need to talk."

"What's up?" asked Dana. "You sound like you've been wrestling with a tiger."

"Yeah, that's a good way to describe how I'm feeling. Today a young African American arrived at the clinic with a dead fetus hanging outside her womb! Dana, she was young and obviously terrified. Why do you suppose she didn't come to us while the baby was still alive?"

Dana waited a long while before responding. "I can only guess why she chose to get rid of the unborn child. Think about it, Phyllis. She's an African-American teenager and probably mortified at the thought of bearing a child without a husband and without family support."

I cupped my hands under my chin, releasing a heavy sigh. "All I could do this morning was grieve for that dead fetus who never had a chance to live, while also sympathizing with a young girl desperate enough to seek an illegal abortion that put her life in jeopardy."

Dana said, "Don't forget that the young girl was also once a baby and deserved to be helped." She stopped long enough for her words to sink in. "As I see it, there are several factors to consider: Was the girl trying to hide her pregnancy from her parents? Had anyone ever educated her on the use of birth control? Finally, how about the male involved? It seems to me he's a vital factor in the equation." Dana hesitated for a few seconds before saying, "After all is said and done, a pregnancy involves one male and one female."

I responded, "If I understand you, Dana, you're saying that having or not having an abortion is a complicated decision and that our duty as physicians is also complicated." I closed our conversation by saying, "Do you suppose someday it will be legal for any woman to get an abortion?"

I told a friend that while I was an intern in Memphis, a man came in with a severe heart attack. He was a farmer whose house had recently burned to a heap of rubble. He reminded me of my dear daddy and his struggles with his heart. For more than two weeks the man continued having cardiac arrests. He set a record in our ICU for having the most CPR attempts. We kept resuscitating him but, ultimately, he died. With his death I found myself in a Cleveland hospital hearing a doctor tell my brother and me, "Your daddy is dead."

"Phyllis," asked my friend, "when did your father die?"

"I was a senior in high school. My mother died seven months earlier than Daddy."

My friend patted me on my arm and assured me. "I've always known you are an amazing young doctor. Now I know your secret. You've turned your losses into stepping stones to support the most vulnerable among us."

A few weeks after I gave birth to my daughter Rachel, I began my OB-GYN duties again. A young lady entered the hospital in labor and was committed to my care. As I began my initial observation of my patient, I soon realized there was not a heartbeat and that the baby was dead.

Pushing back my urge to cry, I said, "I'm so very sorry. Your baby girl died while she was still inside your body." Feeling awkward and not knowing what else to say, I asked, "Would you like to hold your baby?"

The mother reached up and welcomed her lifeless baby girl as she begged, "Oh, Doctor Miller, can't you revive my baby? It's so hard to accept that she's dead!" She sobbed, "We had such great plans for our first child. Can you tell me what happened?"

I was on the brink of tears as I gently told her, "For some unknown reason the baby's umbilical cord became knotted, cutting off the flow of oxygen to the baby. I'm so very sorry this happened."

"Doctor Miller, for nine months I've carried my baby cradled in my body, just waiting for this moment." She sobbed, "And now . . . and now, instead of a party we'll have a funeral."

It was 3:00 a.m. when I changed my scrubs into street clothes and headed home. Upon my arrival I tiptoed over to where Rachel was sound asleep. I picked up the sleeping child and made my way to the rocking chair. Cradling Rachel in my arms, I prayed, "Lord, I feel so helpless! I couldn't do anything to save my patient's baby." I reached down and kissed Rachel's forehead and whispered, "Thank you for giving me a healthy baby."

On one occasion I had an African-American patient, about months into her pregnancy, who arrived on my watch during the night. When I examined her, I discovered that my patient's cervix was widely dilated and that her baby would be born soon if our medical team didn't act quickly.

We immediately performed an emergency cerclage that involved putting a purse string suture around the cervix and cinching it to prevent delivery. This surgery enabled us to hold off our patient's delivery for four more weeks until the birth of her premature baby—and the baby survived!

One day eight years later my office receptionist came to me saying, "There is someone in the waiting room who wants to see you." Upon entering the waiting room, my eyes fell on a young African-American man smiling from ear to ear. Accompanying him was an obviously happy, bouncy little girl who for all purposes was perfectly normal.

"Hello, Doctor Miller," said the young man. "I brought my daughter with me so she could meet the lady who saved her life eight years ago."

I told him, "This is one of the best gifts I've ever received! Thank you so very much for bringing your little girl to meet me."

Through the long years of my tenure of delivering babies, I encountered many cases with birth defects. I found that discovering one's child has a birth defect is heartbreaking but that it sometimes brings out the best in people. This was true of a couple who unexpectedly had a Down's syndrome little girl. The child wasn't expected to survive. Unwilling to accept that ultimatum, though, her parents took her to a hospital in Birmingham where she had a delicate corrective surgery.

Throughout the intervening years I stayed in touch with this family. The child became high-functioning and was mainstreamed in school, became a cheerleader, and was asked by a young male friend to the senior prom. Today she is an adult living independently. Her parents occupy the house on the left of her house, and her grandparents live in the house to the right of where she lives.

I dealt with another Down's syndrome child where the parents initially went into denial that anything was wrong with their baby. Once they were able to accept the fact that their child did have a birth defect, though, they adopted another Down's syndrome child to go with the one they had!

I reached a point in my career where I was beginning to see the babies I delivered grow up, and some of them are having their own babies! It's a weird feeling to deliver a baby for someone who had once been my baby! I'm sometimes stopped around town by a young adult who tells me that I delivered him or her. This is always rewarding. I jokingly tell them it looks like I did a good job since they are smart, pretty, or handsome!

CPSIA information can be obtained
at www.ICGtesting.com
Printed in the USA
LVHW021941201020
669279LV00004B/120

9 781635 281026